THE OLD ONES

THE OLD ONES

INDIANS OF THE AMERICAN SOUTHWEST

BY ROBERT SILVERBERG

Illustrations by Robert Thornton
Photographs by Barbara Silverberg

New York Graphic Society Publishers, Ltd.

Map *by Rafael Palacios*

Library of Congress Catalog No. 65-13542

Published simultaneously in Canada
by McClelland & Stewart Ltd., Toronto

MANUFACTURED IN THE U.S.A.

CONTENTS

	Author's Note	vii
	Introduction: Inscription Rock	11
1	Enter the Spaniards	17
2	In the Beginning	44
3	The People of the Four Corners	55
4	The Early Pueblos	76
5	The Great Years of the Anasazi	95
6	The Apartment-House Builders	116
7	The Cliff-Dwellers	157
8	The Great Trek	174
9	After the Conquest	197
10	The Living Pueblos	220
	Appendix A: Where to See Anasazi Ruins	253
	Appendix B: The Living Pueblos	257
	For Further Reading:	259
	General Indian Background	259
	The Spanish Conquest	260
	The Archaeological Record	261
	The Living Pueblos	263
	Index	265

AUTHOR'S NOTE

THE SPANISH WORD *pueblo* has many meanings: "town," "village," "race," "nation," "populace." In the American Southwest two of these meanings are particularly important. Both will be used in this book.

A "pueblo"—no capital letter—is an Indian village of a particular kind, characterized by flat-roofed buildings plastered with mud. In Arizona and New Mexico today there are twenty-five such pueblos still inhabited by Indians, as well as thousands of ancient ones now in ruin.

A "Pueblo"—capital P—is an inhabitant of a pueblo. The Pueblo Indians actually are divided into many different groups—Hopi, Zuni, Acoma, San Ildefonso, Taos, and so on. The people of the various pueblos differ from one another in language, and, to some extent, in customs, but their ways of life are enough alike to permit them all to be grouped as Pueblos.

THE OLD ONES

INTRODUCTION: INSCRIPTION ROCK

THERE IS A PALE SANDSTONE CLIFF in western New Mexico that has seven centuries of history carved on its face. Some people call it Inscription Rock; others know it by the name the Spaniards gave it, El Morro, "the headland." Near the base of the cliff is a natural rock basin which fills each spring with melting snow to form a pool of fresh water. Travelers passing that way through the desert have stopped at the pool to refresh themselves, and, having stopped, have left a record of their presence there.

The first to come were Indians. The ruins of two Indian pueblos can be seen today at El Morro by those willing to make the 200-foot climb to the top. One pueblo is little more than a mound of weed-covered earth, through which the outlines of rectangular building walls can vaguely be seen. The second, on the other side of a deep-cut box canyon, has been excavated by archaeologists. Its roofless dwellings and storage rooms have been laid bare. So, too, have the round underground rooms known as *kivas,* which have been the centers of Pueblo religious life for more than a thousand years.

The archaeologists tell us that the ruins on top of El Morro were inhabited during the twelfth and thirteenth centuries. At that time each town contained some five hundred rooms, and the buildings rose two or three stories high. Then, more than a century before Columbus sailed westward, the towns atop El Morro were abandoned. We do not know why. The Indians moved away, and their towns fell into ruin.

They left their imprint elsewhere on El Morro. Down the sides of the cliff can be seen notches cut into the rock: footholds for Indians who scrambled down the almost vertical face to get water from the pool below. Near the pool are petroglyphs—the word means "rock carvings"—cut by Indians about the year 1300. They tell a story we can never hope to read. Zigzags and whorls, lizards and stick-figures, the outlines of human hands—were they just decorations, or did they have a deeper meaning?

The carvers of petroglyphs left El Morro. Others came, drawn by the lure of cool water. Spanish conquistadores, hungry for gold, came marching up out of Mexico after they had overthrown Montezuma. In 1540 came Coronado in his gilded armor, and he probably led his troops past El Morro. He and his men were greeted with gifts when they first appeared, but stones and arrows took the place of gifts when the puzzled Indians realized that the strangers had come to conquer.

But Coronado did not conquer. He went back to Mexico a broken, disappointed man who had failed to find the gold he sought. Other Spaniards came. In 1583 an expedition led by Antonio de Espejo journeyed across New Mexico and stopped at El Morro for water. We know this because a member of Espejo's party wrote an account that mentioned "El Estanque del Peñol"—the Pool by the Great Rock.

More Spaniards entered New Mexico. In 1598 came Don Juan de Oñate, with the title of Governor. His mission was to establish Spanish colonies in the new land, and he founded a town called San Gabriel, next door to an Indian pueblo. During his early explorations of the land he governed, Oñate passed El Morro several times, but the first time he recorded his presence was in 1605. He was in search of the ocean that he knew lay somewhere west of New Mexico. He marched into Arizona, past the pueblos of the Hopi Indians, onward to the Colorado River, and from there to the mouth of that river at the Gulf of California. On his way back, Oñate caused this inscription to be carved at the base of El Morro:

PASO POR AQUI EL ADELANTO DON JUAN
DE OÑATE DEL DESCUBRIMIENTO DE LA MAR
DEL SUR A 16 DE ABRIL DE 1605

("Passed by here the Governor Don Juan de Oñate, from the discovery of the Sea of the South, the 16th of April, 1605.")

Oñate's inscription is carved right over an ancient Indian petroglyph. There is something appropriate about that, because Oñate was the first man to bring the Pueblo people under Spanish rule. He and his successors did their best to make good Christians out of the Indians, giving the pueblos the names of saints and baptizing the people.

The Indians humored the Spaniards for a while, but

then the yoke of Christianity became too heavy. They rebelled in 1680 and drove every white man from their land. For twelve years they lived as they had lived in the past, and then the conquerors returned. That too is recorded on El Morro's flank. Diego de Vargas, the conquering general, camped there one night, and ordered it carved that "Here was the General Don Diego de Vargas, who conquered for our Holy Faith, and for the Royal Crown, all of New Mexico at his own expense, year of 1692."

Some of the pueblos remained unconquered: those of the Hopi, in Arizona. In 1716 Don Feliz Martinez passed by El Morro and left an inscription boasting that he was on his way "to the reduction and conquest" of the Hopi. He did not succeed; the Hopi stubbornly refused to yield, and Don Feliz came back again, perhaps glancing ruefully at his inscription as he went by.

There are other Spanish inscriptions on El Morro, the last of them dated 1774. After that a new breed of men came westward, Americans seeking fortunes in the wilderness. A party of traders and trappers rode by in 1829, among them the famous scout, Kit Carson, but they did not leave their names. Twenty years later came James H. Simpson, a lieutenant in the United States Army, who visited El Morro as part of an exploring mission that took him through much of the pueblo country. He and an artist named Richard H. Kern copied the Spanish writing on the rock and left an inscription of their own, the first in English at El Morro: "Lt. J. H. Simpson USA & R. H. Kern Artist visited and copied these inscriptions, September 17th–18th 1849." The man who carved the lines had trouble with his spelling, and left the "r" out of "inscriptions." It had to be patched in with a caret.

Now came a strange expedition indeed. In 1857 another lieutenant, Edward F. Beale, led a camel caravan past El Morro. Jefferson Davis, the Secretary of War in President Buchanan's cabinet, had bought the camels in the Near East, hoping that they would make good pack animals in the deserts of Arizona. The Indians, who had seen their first horses when the Spaniards came, stared in amazement at the weird camels as they clip-clopped by. But the experiment failed.

A year later the wagon-trains of pioneers were rolling westward. Forty families set out for California, were ambushed by Indians in Arizona, and limped back on foot to the town of Albuquerque, New Mexico. They left their names on El Morro: "Williamson," "Holland," "John Udell."

The pioneers went on decorating El Morro all through the nineteenth century. Then the record ends. In 1906 El Morro became a national monument, and today watchful park rangers stand by to keep tourists from adding their names to the roster. There is history enough on El Morro, seven hundred years of it. From ancient petroglyphs to the records of the conquistadores to the signatures of American pioneer settlers, the story of the Southwest is written on the rock.

The people of the pueblos have been forced to share their land with strangers. Once all this vastness belonged to them. They built city after city, skyscrapers of the desert reaching six and seven stories high, elaborate and often strikingly beautiful in their strangeness. Under the bright sun and blue sky of the arid Southwest they developed a complex and fascinating civilization. Peaceful, deeply religious, they tilled their crops and sang their songs and fashioned their marvelous pottery.

Then came the white strangers. Two cultures collided. But the Indians of the pueblos survived the collision. They retained much of their land and kept their ancient ways. Even today, though television sets and shiny automobiles may be seen in the pueblos, the old civilization still exists. Unlike nearly all the other American Indians, the people of the pueblos have endured the coming of the white man and their world is still intact. In their twenty-five villages they worship the old gods and tell the old tales of their ancient heritage.

1

ENTER THE SPANIARDS

THE FIRST STRANGER who came to the pueblos was not a white man at all. He was black, a Moorish slave named Esteban, the property of a Spaniard.

In 1528 an expedition of Spanish adventurers landed on the coast of what is now Florida. After some exploits of remarkable cruelty, they put out to sea in the Gulf of Mexico and their flimsy vessels were scattered by a storm. Esteban and his master were cast up on a beach somewhere near the present-day city of Galveston, Texas. Two others survived also, one of them a certain Cabeza de Vaca. The three Spaniards and the Negro set out on an amazing trek: they decided to walk westward across Texas in the hope of reaching the Spanish settlements in Mexico.

Incredibly, they succeeded. They met with many Indians on their journey. Some were friendly and gave the wanderers food. Others imprisoned them for years at a time. They escaped, fought off heat and cold, starvation, thirst. Without knowing any route through the uncharted lands ahead of them, they fought on. Cabeza de Vaca was the first European to see buffalo—"hunchbacked cows," he called them. In 1536, after eight years of hardship in a trackless wilderness, the four stumbled into a Spanish camp in the Mexican province of Sinaloa, and were quickly taken to Mexico City to tell their astonishing tale to the Spanish viceroy.

During his wanderings, Cabeza de Vaca had heard wonderful stories from the Indians of Texas. They were simple folk themselves, those Indians, but they told the Spaniards of "large and powerful villages, four and five stories high"—the pueblos of New Mexico. They spoke of the wealth of gold that those cities contained; or perhaps Cabeza de Vaca simply imagined that they were telling him of gold.

The Spaniards in Mexico City had been hearing rumors of such golden cities to the north for several years. A half-breed named Tejo had spread tales of chieftains ornamented in gold and silver. Cabeza de Vaca's story seemed to confirm what Tejo had told.

Even wealthy Mexico did not hold enough of the yellow metal to satisfy the Spaniards; they began to plan an expedition into the unknown northern land. Mendoza, the Spanish viceroy, asked an Italian-born priest, Fray (friar) Marcos de Niza, to make a reconnaissance mission in advance of a major invasion.

The obvious man to take as a guide was Cabeza de Vaca, whose experience in dealing with strange Indian tribes was unequaled. But he had had enough of that neighborhood, and had headed for South America on another adventure. The slave, Esteban, was still in Mexico

City. Viceroy Mendoza bought him and sent him off with Fray Marcos.

They left on March 7, 1539. Accompanying Fray Marcos and Esteban were a monk named Fray Onorato (who fell sick almost at once and had to be left behind), and a few Mexican Indians who had learned Spanish and embraced Christianity. A forbidding desert and lofty mountains lay ahead; beyond were the fabled cities, which were said to be seven in number.

Fray Marcos sent Esteban forward as an advance scout. His task was to make contact with the Indians along the route, win their friendship, and arrange for provisions. The Negro revelled in his assignment. Up till now he had been only a lowly slave; suddenly he was an explorer, a pioneer, a trailblazer.

Marching jauntily, confidently, Esteban plunged into the unknown. He met Indians and awed them with the blackness of his skin. They had never seen such a creature before. Esteban the slave became Esteban the god. He decked himself in feathers and bells; he covered himself with the precious blue-green stones called turquoises that the Indians gave him; he acquired a sacred rattle and carried it like a scepter.

Fray Marcos had instructed Esteban to send back messengers bearing news of the Seven Cities. If they were plain and poor, Esteban was to send a cross the length of a man's hand. If the cities were large and appeared wealthy, Esteban was to send a cross twice that length. And if the new lands were greater and richer than those of Mexico, he was to send back a cross even larger.

On the fourth day after Esteban had gone ahead, the

first messenger returned to Fray Marcos. He was carrying a cross as tall as a man. The Seven Cities, then, were treasure-troves more glittering than those of the conquered Aztecs! Fray Marcos hurried forward. He found even larger crosses set up along the trail. Another messenger appeared, with word from Esteban that the cities were those of a province called Cibola, and that they were vast and mighty cities of a rich and populous kingdom.

Hurrying along, Fray Marcos passed through the small Indian villages in northern Mexico and asked the inhabitants what they knew of the Seven Cities of Cibola. They told him of the houses and streets, of the market-places and plazas. Some of the houses, they said, were ten stories high. He asked if the people of those cities "had wings to mount up" to the highest stories, and they laughed and told him that the people of Cibola used ladders.

The priest crossed what is now the border separating Mexico from Arizona. He journeyed through the Gila lowlands and ascended the great plateau that occupies so much of the American Southwest. Friendly Indians escorted him, hunting deer, rabbits, and partridges for him. Then, in May, there appeared one of the Mexican Indians who had gone forward with Esteban. The messenger, Fray Marcos wrote, "came in a great fright, having his face and body all covered with sweat, and showing exceeding sadness in his countenance."

He bore grim news. Esteban was dead.

Esteban had reached one of the Seven Cities of Cibola —probably Hawikuh, a pueblo of Zuni Indians. Adorned with feathers, carrying his magic rattles, followed by a train of awed Indians who regarded him as a supernatural being, Esteban had presented himself at Hawikuh. From the lofty towers of the pueblo, its inhabitants looked out and saw a man of the Old World for the first time.

Esteban demanded admittance. He sent a messenger into Hawikuh bearing one of the magic gourd rattles he had acquired along the way. But what was "magic" to the primitive Indians of the border country meant nothing to the people of Hawikuh. An elder of the pueblo hurled the gourd to the ground and told Esteban's messenger to get out.

Too confident, Esteban insisted on entering the pueblo. Warriors met him and warned him away. He laughed at them and asked for a tribute of turquoise. Instead they seized him and took away his accumulation of treasures. They threw him into a house outside the pueblo and kept him under guard, without food.

The wisest men of Hawikuh came to question him. They asked the black man if he had any "brothers." Yes, he said, and they were white. That made the elders suspicious. Esteban went on to say that a great many white men were on their way, well armed, "to instruct them in divine matters."

They could not understand how a black man could be the messenger of white men, and, having a perfectly good religion of their own, they were in no need of instruction. Furthermore, Esteban had arrived carrying the trinkets of hostile Indian tribes. All these things, wrote a Spanish chronicler a few years later, "made them think that he must be a spy or a guide from some nations that wished to come and conquer them." So when Esteban tried to run away one morning, they killed him. His body was torn to pieces and his possessions divided. One man of Hawikuh took four green plates, crockery that Esteban had carried from Mexico. The Indians who had accompanied Esteban were allowed to go free.

Fray Marcos, following Esteban's trail, feared to go ahead. He was alone now except for his Indian escort, and it seemed certain suicide to continue on to Cibola. Timidly he went forward until he came to a hill that gave him a distant view of the city where Esteban had perished. Then, after a single glimpse of the promised land, Fray Marcos hurried back to Mexico to make his report to Viceroy Mendoza.

The city, he wrote, "is situated on a plain at the foot of a round hill, and makes show to be a fair city, and is better seated than any I have seen in these parts. The houses are . . . all made of stone with many stories, and flat roofs." He did not actually say he had seen gold in Cibola, but he quoted a native report: "I was told that there is much gold there and that the natives make it into vessels and jewels for their ears, and into little blades with which they wipe away their sweat."

The Spaniards seethed with gold-hunger. Swiftly, on the strength of what Fray Marcos had seen from a far-off vantage point, Mendoza equipped a large expedition. He placed thirty-year-old Francisco Vasquez de Coronado at its head.

Coronado was a handsome Spanish aristocrat who had come to Mexico to make his fortune. He had done well so far, having married a beautiful heiress with extensive properties. Intelligent, ambitious, Coronado was eager to add to his wealth and to enhance the glory of Spain. But he lacked that streak of cruelty that marked most of his countrymen. He was not by nature capable of committing the atrocities and acts of treachery that had marked the Spanish conquests of Mexico and Peru.

The expedition departed early in 1540. Pedro de Castañeda, a soldier in Coronado's army, wrote an account of the journey twenty years later in which he said "they had on this expedition the most brilliant company ever collected in the Indies to go in search of new lands." Coronado had about three hundred Spaniards, many slaves, a thousand Indian servants, fifteen hundred horses, mules, and cattle. The soldiers were armed with swords, daggers, and lances; twenty-seven had arquebuses, those clumsy ancestors of the rifle, and nineteen had crossbows.

Coronado himself was a magnificent sight as the expedition departed. His armor was gilded; two plumes sprang from his gleaming helmet. With him rode Fray Marcos de Niza as his guide.

Fray Marcos had said the route to Cibola was an easy one. But what a lone friar and a few Indians had found easy, a full-scale army found all but impassable. Leading an advance party of one hundred, Coronado struggled through the mountains and through the desert wastes. The Spaniards reached Arizona gaunt and weary. Many horses died. Rations ran low.

The explorers went up the Gila River and came to a ruined pueblo that the Aztecs of Mexico called Chichilticalli, or the Red House, because it was built of red mud. Rumor said it was a magnificent palace, but the Red House did not live up to its advance description; Castañeda called it a "tumble-down house without any roof," though he said "it appeared to have been a strong place at some former time when it was inhabited."

But if the Red House was disappointing, Cibola was an utter catastrophe. The first village that Coronado's men came to was Hawikuh, which the Spaniards called Cibola after the entire province. They reached it on July 7, 1540. At a distance it seemed impressive, four stories high, its plastered walls glittering in the sun. But, Castañeda tells us, "When they saw the first village, which was Cibola, such were the curses that some hurled at Friar Marcos that I pray God may protect him from them. It is a little unattractive village, looking as if it had been crumpled up all together. There are mansions in New Spain [Mexico] which make a better appearance at a distance."

Fray Marcos must have paled with fear at his first close look at a city of Cibola. Where was the gold? Where was the splendor? What had he led the expedition into? "It is a village of about two hundred warriors," wrote Castañeda, "and is three and four stories high, with the houses small and having only a few rooms, and without courtyards."

The chief hunger of the Spaniards by this time was for food, not gold. Coronado and his men had nearly exhausted their provisions in crossing the desert. He sent a party ahead to make peaceful overtures and negotiate for food. The people of the pueblo, who had put Esteban to death the year before, still wanted no dealings with the strangers. They drove the Spaniards away with arrows. It was not really in character for them, since they had a long tradition of peace, these gentle and noble city-dwelling Indians. But fear possessed them.

Coronado did not want to begin his career in Cibola with an act of war, but he desperately needed food. He ordered his men to attack. The Pueblo warriors put up a sturdy resistance against the weakened invaders. The only entrance to the pueblo was a narrow one, well guarded. The Indians mounted their flat rooftops and hurled down "countless great stones." Coronado, in his brilliant gilded armor, was an easy target. He was knocked down twice by stones and hit in the foot by an arrow. Within an hour, though, the Pueblos yielded, and the Spaniards burst into Hawikuh. They seized the supply of corn stored in the pueblo and made themselves masters of the village.

No gold, no silver. The chagrined Fray Marcos quickly found an excuse to depart for Mexico City. His health had been poor, and he had suffered greatly on the journey across the desert; but perhaps he also thought it wise to remove himself from the scene before some angry conquistador attacked him. Coronado wrote to Mendoza that Fray Marcos "has not told the truth in a single thing he said." The friar had not really lied, though; he had simply been too optimistic.

The Zuni village of Hawikuh was a typical New Mexican pueblo. It was a huge apartment house of hundreds of small rooms clustered close together. Built of slabs of stone mortared by mud, it rose in terrace after terrace to a height of several stories. Its people were farmers, raising corn, beans, and squash. The women made excellent pottery. The men tilled the fields. The people were placid, well-behaved, orderly. They were not at all like the fierce Aztecs of Mexico, who gloried in bloody human sacrifice.

Castañeda wrote, "They do not have chiefs as in New Spain, but are ruled by a council of the oldest men. They have priests who preach to them, whom they call *papas* [a Zuni word meaning 'elder brothers']. These are the elders. . . . They tell them how they are to live, and I believe that they give certain commandments for them to keep, for there is no drunkenness among them nor wickedness nor sacrifices, neither do they eat human flesh nor steal, but they are usually at work."

Coronado was particularly impressed with the efficient way the women of Hawikuh ground corn. He wrote to Mendoza in August, "They have the very best arrangement and machinery for grinding that was ever seen. One of these Indian women here will grind as much as four of the Mexicans." And Castañeda described the corn-grinding process in detail. The women used sandstone slabs as their grinding stones, to which the Spaniards gave an Aztec name, *metate*. They milled the corn by grinding it against the metate with a smaller stone called a *mano* (Spanish for "hand"). Castañeda wrote:

"They keep the separate houses where they prepare the food for eating and where they grind the meal, very clean. This is a separate room or closet, where they have a trough with three stones fixed in stiff clay. Three women go in here, each one having a stone, with which one of them breaks the corn, the next grinds it, and the third grinds it again. They take off their shoes, do up their hair, shake their clothes, and cover their heads before they enter the door. A man sits at the door playing on a flute while they grind. They move the stones to the music and sing together. They grind a large quantity at one time, because they make all their bread of meal soaked in warm water, like wafers."

Having been defeated in a single battle, the Zuni of Hawikuh did not attempt further resistance. Peacefully they accepted the presence of the Spaniards among them. Coronado's men prowled the pueblo, still dreaming of coming upon hidden storerooms packed ten feet deep with gold and emeralds and rubies. They found nothing but corn and beans, and they were bitterly disappointed. Many talked of deserting Coronado and turning back.

Coronado clung to the hope of finding treasure somewhere. He encouraged the natives to tell him about other inhabited cities. They informed him that there was a province called Tusayan, a few days' journey to the northwest, which had seven villages, much like those of Cibola except that they were built of mud instead of stone.

Tusayan did not seem promising, but Coronado decided to investigate. He dispatched a party of about twenty men, commanded by Captain Pedro de Tovar and led by Zuni guides. Tovar and his band found Tusayan to be a group of pueblos inhabited by the Indians known today as the Hopi. The Hopi, living in seven villages on four mesas in otherwise deserted country, had already heard of the Spanish invasion of Cibola. News traveled mysteriously fast in Pueblo country. The Hopi had been told that the Spaniards were very fierce, and that they traveled "on animals which ate people." (Horses were unknown in the New World when the Europeans discovered it. They had become extinct in the Americas thousands of years before.)

Tovar slipped into Tusayan under cover of darkness.

He and his men hid below one of the Hopi mesas, but were discovered in the morning. Hopi warriors armed with bows and wooden clubs came down from their village. They drew a line across the trail with sacred cornmeal, and quietly informed the Spaniards they must not cross it. A parley followed, but the visitors grew impatient. During the conversation, carried on partly in sign language and partly through a native interpreter, one of the Hopi lost his temper and struck a Spanish horse with his club.

Friar Juan de Padilla, a priest who had been a soldier in his youth, grew angry at this. "Why are we here?" he shouted. The soldiers sounded their battle cry of "Santiago!" and charged the Hopi with lance and sword. The Indians fled into their pueblo atop the mesa. Soon after, they made their submission, offering gifts of turquoise, corn, firewood, cotton cloth, and the highly edible nuts of the pinyon pine.

Tovar inspected the village, which was the Hopi pueblo of Awatobi, and found that its people were much like those of Hawikuh: basically peaceful farmers, who lived quiet, law-abiding lives in their flat-topped mud-plastered houses. Again, no gold, no silver, no metal of any kind, no precious stones except a few turquoises.

The expedition returned to Coronado, who was still at Hawikuh. Wishing to know more about Tusayan, Coronado sent out a second party under Don Garcia Lopez de Cardenas. He returned to Awatobi, was received amiably by the Indians, and was told of a great river to the west. Cardenas went in search of it. In the heat of summer he crossed the Arizona desert and came at last to a region described by Castañeda as "elevated and full of low twisted pines, very cold, and lying open toward the north." Then they saw the river. They were on the rim of a vast gash in the surface of the earth, many miles wide. The river flowed far below. It seemed to be only a tiny stream, though the Indians had said it was "half a league wide."

Three of the most agile Spaniards clambered down the side of the canyon toward the distant river. They hoped to bring water back; but about four o'clock in the afternoon of the day they set out they returned with empty canteens. They had not even come close to the river. Castañeda wrote, "They could not reach the bottom because of the many obstacles they met, for what from the top seemed easy, was not so; on the contrary, it was rough and difficult. They said that they had been down about a third of the way and that the river seemed very large from the place which they reached. . . . From the top they could make out, apart from the canyon, some small boulders which seemed to be as high as a man. Those who went down and reached them swore that they were taller than the great tower of Seville." The tower they referred to was the bell tower of Seville Cathedral, which is 275 feet high. Cardenas' men had been the first Europeans to enter the Grand Canyon.

While these parties were out exploring, Coronado and most of his men remained at Hawikuh, resting after their arduous journey from Mexico. One day some Indians from another pueblo arrived to see the Spaniards. They were from the pueblo of Pecos, some two hundred miles to the east. (Somehow the Spaniards heard the name as

"Cicuye," and that is how it is recorded in their annals.)

The men from Pecos were led by an Indian whom the Spaniards nicknamed Bigotes ("Whiskers") because he wore a long mustache. Bigotes told Coronado that Pecos wished to show its friendship to the newcomers. He offered presents of shields and tanned hides and headpieces, in return for which Coronado gave him glass dishes, some pearls, and little bells. Bigotes invited the Spaniards to visit his country.

Coronado chose an officer named Hernando de Alvarado, and sent him with twenty companions to make an eighty-day exploration of the region around Cicuye. In five days, Alvarado came to a pueblo atop a mesa more than three hundred feet high. The only way up was by a narrow staircase cut into the rock.

This was the pueblo of Acoma, which still is inhabited. At that time its people had a sinister reputation; according to Castañeda they "were robbers, feared by the whole country round about." He noted that "the village was very strong, because it was up on a rock out of reach, having steep sides in every direction, and so high that it was a very good musket that could throw a ball as high." Led by curiosity, perhaps, the Acomans had rashly come down from their impregnable fortress to get a close look at Alvarado and his men; and though they had descended with the intention of doing battle, they quickly decided against it. Instead of fighting, they made a formal agreement of peace with the Spaniards and offered presents of turkeys, bread, pinyon nuts, cornmeal, and corn. But it was not a treaty that they intended to keep.

Alvarado continued into the province he called Tiguex. Here, in the region around the modern city of Albuquerque, there were many pueblos. Because Bigotes was with them, the Spaniards were received hospitably, and Alvarado sent word to Coronado that he should consider spending the winter in one of the twelve pueblos of Tiguex. Then Alvarado moved on. Five days east of Tiguex lay Pecos, or Cicuye. Castañeda's account declares that it was "a very strong village four stories high. The people came out from the village with signs of joy to welcome Hernando de Alvarado and their captain, and brought them into the town with drums and pipes something like flutes, of which they have a great many. They made many presents of cloth and turquoises, of which there are quantities in that region."

At Pecos the Spaniards met an Indian who was to cause them enormous trouble. He was no Pueblo, but came from the lands to the east; possibly he was a Pawnee. The Spaniards called him Turk, because, says Castañeda, "he looked like one."

Turk told the Spaniards glowing tales of the eastern land. He described the great herds of buffalo that roamed the plains, and that interested Alvarado, but not nearly so much as some of the other things Turk said. He spoke of "a river, flowing through the plains, which was two leagues wide, with fish as large as horses and a great number of very large canoes with sails, carrying more than twenty oarsmen on each side." The nobles of that region ate from "pitchers, dishes and bowls made of gold." And, said Turk, "the lord of that land took his siesta under a large tree from which hung numerous golden jingle bells, and he was pleased as they played in the wind."

The buffalo herds were there, all right, and the great

river, which was probably the Missouri or the Mississippi. But the gold was a fantasy. The honest Bigotes told Alvarado as much, insisting that Turk was lying. Turk claimed that he had given Bigotes golden bracelets as gifts. When Bigotes denied it, Alvarado had him seized and tortured, but still he maintained that he knew nothing of gold or golden bracelets. Inflamed by reawakened greed, Alvarado put Bigotes and another important man of Pecos in chains, and took them back to Tiguex as prisoners.

The winter was approaching. Snow was falling heavily. Coronado chose as his winter camp the pueblo of Puaray, which he called Tiguex, after the name applied to the entire group of pueblos in the district. He and his army took up residence within Puaray. There, Coronado listened again to Turk's tales of gold, and to Bigotes' denials.

This pueblo of Tiguex or Puaray, which was near the modern town of Bernalillo, was different from the others to the west, in that it was built not of stone covered with plaster, but of dried mud that had been shaped and pressed into the form of walls. Castañeda observed that "they collect great heaps of thyme and rushes and set them on fire; when the mass is reduced to ashes and charcoal they cast a great quantity of earth and water upon it and mix the whole together. They knead this stuff into round lumps, which they learn to dry and use instead of stone." The Spaniards called this kind of construction *adobe,* from the Spanish word *adobar,* meaning "to plaster."

Tiguex had welcomed the Spaniards eagerly enough, but very shortly there was trouble. The imprisonment of

Bigotes caused resentment, for he was an important man of a neighboring pueblo. Some of Coronado's soldiers behaved in a swaggering, overbearing way, taking clothing and blankets from the Indians. There was friction, and suddenly a revolt. The men of Tiguex started a stampede among the Spanish horses and mules, and many of the valuable pack animals were lost. The invaders were driven from the pueblos where they had taken up quarters. They fought back, but one pueblo held out for a siege lasting fifty days. Cardenas, the discoverer of the Grand Canyon, gave the Pueblos a taste of customary Spanish methods of warfare; he invited them to surrender, guaranteeing not to harm them, and then butchered more than a hundred as a warning to the rest.

By the spring of 1541 the villages of the Tiguex area were under Coronado's control again. But the Spanish record in New Mexico was now deeply stained with Pueblo blood, and the bitterness was long-lasting.

Turk continued to entertain Coronado with tales of Quivira, the wondrous land of gold and buffalo. Drawn by the golden lure, Coronado set forth from Tiguex early in May with Turk as his guide. After releasing Bigotes at Pecos, the Spaniards followed Turk eastward toward what is now Texas. They came upon "people who lived like Arabs and who are called Querechos"—nomad Indians of the plains, Apache or perhaps Tonkawa. They saw the buffalo, too, uncountable thousands of the bulky brown beasts. But there was no gold. On and on and on they marched, engulfed in an immense country with no roads, no landmarks, no boundaries.

Where was the gold? Coronado grew weary of the eastward trek. Another Indian in the party said that Turk had misled them, that golden Quivira lay to the north, not to the east. So Turk was clapped in chains and the Spaniards returned to Tiguex and began all over again, this time heading toward the plains of the north. But this new venture was another disaster. Coronado plunged deep into what now is Kansas, on a journey of more than a thousand miles. He found rich black farmland, yes, and buffalo "as large as anyone could imagine," and fertile forests rich with "grapes and mulberries and plums." These riches meant nothing; it was only the yellow metal that drew them on.

At length the Spaniards put Turk to the torture, and he told the truth. In Castañeda's words, "He said that the people at Cicuye had asked him to lead them off onto the plains and lose them, so that the horses would die when their provisions gave out, and they would be so weak that if they ever returned they could be killed without any trouble. . . . As for the gold, he did not know where there was any of it."

The deceitful Turk was put to death. The dejected Spaniards made the long journey back to Tiguex. They passed the winter of 1541–42 there, and in the spring Coronado decided to return to Mexico. Two Franciscan friars, the warlike Juan de Padilla and another named Luis, asked to remain to convert the natives to Christianity. Coronado left them. Friar Luis went to Pecos, Friar Juan to search for Quivira, and both men met swift martyrdom in their attempts to interfere with the Pueblo religion.

Coronado's return was sad. He fell from his horse and

was badly injured, and he was broken in health and spirit by the time he reached Mexico City. The general who had departed in gilded armor came back empty-handed and ill, and was coldly received by the disappointed viceroy. Coronado's remaining years were few and dark, plagued by lawsuits and bitter accusations.

FOR FORTY YEARS the pueblos were at peace, and perhaps the visit of Coronado came to seem to them like no more than a bad dream. In Mexico, though, there were still some who sought to add the Pueblo land to the Spanish domain.

In 1581 Fray Augustin Rodriguez obtained permission to enter New Mexico as a missionary. With two other friars, a supporting party of nine soldiers, and sixteen Indian servants, Rodriguez followed the river already known as the Rio Grande until he came to the southernmost pueblos, now deserted, in the region of Socorro. They went on to the Tiguex pueblos and visited Puaray, Coronado's winter headquarters forty years before. They traveled as far west as Acoma and the Zuni villages, but made no converts. One of the friars was killed when he set out alone to return to Mexico; soon after, the military escort left Rodriguez and his companion, Fray Francisco Lopez, at Puaray. The soldiers went back to Mexico and one of them, Gallegos, wrote a report describing the customs and clothing of the Pueblos. "Some adorn themselves with painted cotton pieces of cloth three handspans long and two thirds as wide. . . . Over this they wear, fastened at the shoulders, a blanket of the same material, painted with many figures and colors. It reaches to their knees like the clothing of the Mexicans. Some, in fact most of them, wear cotton shirts, hand painted and embroidered, that are very charming. They wear shoes. Below the waist the women wear cotton skirts, colored and embroidered, and above, a blanket of the same material, painted and worked like those used by the men."

Fathers Rodriguez and Lopez met martyrdom at Puaray. This was discovered the following year, 1582, when another expedition led by Antonio de Espejo and Fray Bernadino Beltran went north to find and rescue them. The party numbered about twenty. When Espejo and his men came to Puaray and learned of the murder of the friars, the people fled to the mountains, fearing they would be punished. "We tried to bring them back peacefully," Espejo wrote, "but they refused to return. In their houses we found a large quantity of maize, beans, gourds, many turkeys, and many ores of different colors."

The expedition's purpose had been achieved. But Espejo's curiosity drove him on. This wealthy merchant, deeming it "a good opportunity for me to serve his Majesty by visiting and discovering those lands so new and remote," explored the region around Tiguex, then headed west. He came to the lofty Acoma pueblo and was received by its people with surprising friendliness. After three days there, during which time the Acomans "in our honor performed a very ceremonious dance, the people coming out in fine array and . . . performing many juggling feats, some of them very clever, with live snakes," Espejo journeyed onward past El Morro to the Zuni pueblos.

There were six of them, not the seven that Fray Marcos had heard of long ago. (Today five are in ruins, and the sixth is known as Zuni.) Here in Esteban's Cibola, Espejo discovered three Mexican Indians who had been part of Coronado's expedition. He had left them there in 1540, and now, in 1583, they had forgotten their native language and barely remembered their own names. They told Espejo of the journeys of Tovar and Cardenas, and spurred him on with the old dream of gold.

He followed Tovar's path to the Hopi mesas. There was no gold, of course—only gifts of gaily colored cotton blankets. After a futile search for the precious metal in central Arizona, he went back to Zuni, and then, his thirst for adventure still unslaked, returned to the Rio Grande to explore the pueblos north of the modern city of Santa Fe.

Espejo's report declared that the Pueblo Indians "are an intelligent and well-governed people, with pueblos well formed and houses well arranged, and from what we could understand from them, anything regarding good government they will learn quickly." He expressed the belief that "many rich mines" existed in their country, a belief that was only a hope.

The Spanish authorities began to think seriously of founding a colony in New Mexico. In 1590 an enthusiastic officer named Gaspar Castaño de Sosa organized a group of 170 men and women and led them into the land of the Pueblos without bothering to get official authorization. He came to Pecos, was greeted by arrows, and forced the inhabitants to submit. Entering the pueblo, Sosa inspected it carefully. He paid particular attention to the circular underground chambers that we know today by the Hopi term of *kivas,* meaning "old houses." The kiva is the religious and social center of the village, but Sosa believed that these well-plastered chambers were places of refuge during cold weather. In this he followed Coronado, who had referred to kivas by the Spanish word *estufas,* "ovens."

Sosa got as far north as Taos, the northernmost pueblo along the Rio Grande, in the course of his explorations. He visited many pueblos and conquered them all without much difficulty. But in the midst of his triumphal procession he was overtaken by soldiers sent from Mexico to arrest him for trying to found a colony without permission. He was taken into custody, and all the colonists were returned to Mexico.

That false start was followed by a more successful expedition a few years later. An energetic, dynamic man named Juan de Oñate finally established a permanent Spanish base in New Mexico.

Oñate belonged to a family that had been prominent in the conquest of Mexico, and his wife was the granddaughter of Cortés and the great-granddaughter of the Aztec monarch Montezuma. In 1595 the Spanish government had awarded Oñate the privilege of founding a colony in New Mexico. Political wrangling delayed his departure from Mexico until February, 1598. The colonizing party consisted of four hundred men, women, and children, with more than eighty baggage carts and seven thousand head of cattle.

The Spanish no longer were coming to New Mexico by way of Arizona. They had found an eastern route out of Mexico via the Rio Conchos and the Rio Grande. Their crossing into what is now New Mexico was at the site of present-day El Paso, Texas, and near there Oñate formally took possession "of all the kingdoms and provinces of

New Mexico" in the name of King Philip III of Spain. Soon he was at the southernmost of the pueblos, the now-abandoned Trenaquel.

The Spaniards were welcomed with feasts and celebrations. While the gentle Indians were displaying their hospitality, a surprising thing happened. One approached Oñate and shouted, in Spanish, "Thursday! Friday! Saturday! Sunday!"

The Spaniards were astounded. They begged the Indian to say something else, but he had exhausted his Spanish vocabulary. After long questioning, the man pointed to the north and said, "Thomas and Cristobal." Evidently there were men with Christian names living north of Trenaquel, perhaps survivors of some earlier expedition.

Oñate hurried on up the Rio Grande, which then as now was lined with pueblos. At Puaray they were again received in a friendly manner, and quartered in rooms that had been freshly whitewashed. The next day, though, when the whitewash dried, they saw that it covered painted scenes depicting the martyrdom of Rodriguez and his companion in 1582. The Indians had tactfully covered the murals to avoid offending their new guests.

Men of Puaray led Oñate to a nearby pueblo where Cristobal and Thomas were dwelling. They turned out to be Indians of Mexico who had accompanied Castaño de Sosa on his expedition eight years before. They had remained in the pueblo voluntarily and had married Pueblo women. Oñate found them highly useful, for they spoke the local language as well as Spanish, and made excellent interpreters.

The Spaniards visited a number of the pueblos in the

Rio Grande region. At each, Oñate announced that the land now belonged to King Philip of Spain, and he invited the leading men of each pueblo to pay homage to the Spanish king and to embrace the teachings of Christ. The Indians obligingly agreed, probably without any real understanding of Oñate's demands.

Gaspar de Villagrá, a soldier in Oñate's entourage, wrote a lengthy account of this expedition. Like the other chroniclers, he was favorably impressed both by the pueblos and by the Pueblos. The pueblos, he wrote, "are all well built with straight, well-squared walls. Their towns have no defined streets. Their houses are three, five, six and even seven stories high, with many windows and terraces. . . . The men spin and weave and the women cook, build the houses, and keep them in repair. They dress in garments of cotton cloth, and the women wear beautiful shawls of many colors. They are quiet, peaceful people of good appearance and excellent physique, alert and intelligent."

On July 11, 1598, Oñate reached the pueblo of Caypa, a short distance west of the Rio Grande, and selected it as the site for the colony. He gave Caypa the Christian name of San Juan, by which it is still known today, and early in August construction began on a Spanish village, San Gabriel, not far from the pueblo. (San Gabriel was destined to be inhabited for only a few years. After centuries of neglect, it was excavated by archaeologists from the University of New Mexico in 1960. The foundations of Oñate's settlement were discovered in the back yard of a farmer named Montoya, who allowed the archaeologists to dig.)

With the colony established, Oñate set out to explore the rest of the countryside. He sent a party of sixty men commanded by Vicente de Zaldivar to visit Pecos and examine the buffalo plains to the east. Oñate himself went southeast, discovered valuable salt deposits, then turned westward in quest of the "South Sea," where he hoped to find pearls. He passed Zuni and entered the Hopi country; a scouting party continued onward, deeper into Arizona, and found rich silver mines.

In November, 1598, Oñate's second-in-command, Juan de Zaldivar (brother of Vicente), set out to join Oñate in his expedition to the South Sea. Zaldivar and his companions stopped at the mesa-top pueblo of Acoma. Oñate had been there a short time before, unfurling the Spanish flag and proclaiming the sovereignty of King Philip and of Christ. The Acomans had been outwardly friendly then, but after Oñate's departure, they had decided on a campaign of resistance.

They greeted Juan de Zaldivar pleasantly, offering gifts and supplies. Lulled by this reception, about twenty Spaniards climbed to the top of the 357-foot-high mesa to collect provisions. They were suddenly surrounded by the treacherous Acomans, who attacked savagely. Many of the Spaniards were slain by Indian spears and clubs. Juan de Zaldivar fought heroically, but finally perished. Five Spaniards still remained. Villagrá's narrative tells us that the five, "having fought long and fiercely, and having bested their assailants at every turn, dealing blows right and left, fought their way to the edge of the rock. Here one and all they leaped to either life or death. . . . Truly it was a miracle that they should escape alive." The miracle occurred. The five men dropped more than three hundred feet, but landed in thick drifts of desert sand that had collected at the base of the mesa. One was killed when he struck the side of the rock; the other four were stunned, but survived the fall and were carried off by Spaniards who had escaped less spectacularly earlier in the conflict.

Two months later, Vicente de Zaldivar came to Acoma to avenge his brother's death. The battle lasted three days, and was marked by extraordinary feats of heroism on both sides. At length the Spaniards, outnumbered but more skilled in warfare, prevailed. Hundreds of Acomans were slaughtered, and the survivors surrendered. The vengeful Spaniards put the pueblo to the torch, and it was completely destroyed; but when the ashes had cooled the remaining Acomans returned and began to rebuild their village. A handful of Indians are still living there today, high above the flat desert west of Albuquerque.

Oñate had not managed to reach the South Sea while the Acoma uprising was taking place. Nor did Vicente de Zaldivar get there on his expedition in 1599. In 1601 Oñate planned one more attempt, but changed his mind at the last moment and went northeast instead, as far as the present location of Wichita, Kansas. He carried out his western expedition at last in 1604, following the Colorado River to the Gulf of California, which he called the South Sea, and it was on his return from that enterprise in April, 1605, that he carved his famous inscription on El Morro. He ruled New Mexico until 1608; then he became entangled in the intrigues of envious countrymen, and fell from power.

Though his own career had ended in failure, Oñate had achieved Spain's goal. He had established Spanish rule over the country of the pueblos, a rule that would endure —except for the years of rebellion from 1680 to 1692— for more than two hundred years. The Pueblos, some 20,000 in all, occupying about seventy towns at the time of the conquest, became subjects of the Spanish crown.

And so the Pueblos, who had never known masters, lost their freedom. The Spaniards did not know, and probably did not care, that they had conquered a civilization that was as ancient as it was rich and complex. The people of the mud villages had had a glorious past, but it remained for later men to rediscover and interpret the story of that remarkable heritage.

2

IN THE BEGINNING

THE BEGINNINGS are shrouded by the mists of time. Where does the story start? There were men, or creatures akin to men, living in Asia and Africa perhaps a million years ago. But the Americas knew no human footfall. While our remote ancestors were dwelling in steaming Javanese jungles, while they were shivering in the caves of Europe, the New World had no men.

Then bands of straggling hunters began to filter into North America. They came, a few dozen at a time, out of Asia, crossing the 56-mile Bering Strait. The migration was slow, lasting thousands of years. Two virgin continents awaited them, and they drifted unhurriedly down through Alaska and Canada into the Americas, all the way to the tip of Cape Horn.

They were hunters. They knew nothing of farming, and lived by killing the giant beasts that then roamed our continent. These first Americans arrived, so we think today, some twenty or thirty thousand years ago. In the Southwest they hunted mastodons and mammoths, camels, bison, horses—a whole horde of animals later to become extinct in the New World. They varied their diet, perhaps, by gathering wild berries and roots, but they had no fields, no farms, no villages. They were nomads, drifting where the game went, killing and roasting and eating, and then moving on.

We know very little about those early men. With one or two possible exceptions, we have never found any of their skeletal remains. They left no dwellings for archaeologists to find, no works of art, no signs of their presence but one. We have found the points of their spears or arrows, and we have found the charred bones of the animals they killed and cooked.

So we recognize them only by their weapons. Each group of hunters had its own style of weapon point, and each style remained in fashion for thousands of years at a time, until replaced by a newer kind. We call the earliest Americans by names derived from the modern sites where their weapons were found. Thus we have Sandia Man, dating from about 25,000 B.C., who made crude-looking points lopsided at the base. We have Folsom Man, who roamed the plains between 20,000 and 10,000 B.C., and left behind great numbers of attractive little points with narrow grooves running vertically up their faces. There are the Yuma Points, and the Gypsum Cave Points, and the Clovis Points, and others as well.

About eight thousand years ago a catastrophe struck the world of the hunters. The giant mammals that were their prey began to die out. The ground sloth and the great bison, the saber-toothed cat and the dire wolf, the camel and horse, the mammoth and mastodon, all vanished. We are not sure why, but we think the climate was an important factor. North America had been a moist, cool place in the days of Folsom Man. Now it grew drier and warmer. Deserts appeared in the Southwest where thickly forested land had been before. The change of habitat seems to have been too much for the big animals, and they became extinct.

The hunting tribes left the Southwest and followed the game inland. They abandoned the now arid Southwest to a different sort of people whose lives did not revolve around the killing of big beasts. These were a folk who began to settle in southeastern Arizona while it was still occupied by the hunters and roamed by camels and mammoths.

Though the climate was cool and moist when these people came, it soon changed. The hunters departed, but this other culture, though simple and nomadic, was able to adapt itself to the new conditions. Its people depended for their food supply upon the gathering of seeds, berries, and roots, and the hunting of small game such as rabbits, prairie dogs, and doves. They learned to build crude shelters for themselves, and settled down.

Archaeologists call this new culture of foragers and food-gatherers the Cochise culture, because the first evidence of its existence was unearthed near the town of Cochise, Arizona, in 1926. The Cochise people may have begun their way of life about ten thousand years ago; certainly they were occupying their territory by 6000 B.C. Scientists using the carbon-14 method of dating, an extremely exact technique developed in the late 1940's, have dated one Cochise site at 6240 B.C.

These simple food-gatherers were not yet farmers, but

they did make one significant invention. Archaeologists have found metates and manos at the Cochise sites, indicating that they ground the roots and seeds they collected. These milling stones are important, because they show that the Cochise people were taking the first steps toward controlling their environment. By grinding their seeds and grains and roots, they made available to themselves certain types of food that would not otherwise have been edible.

The earliest Cochise people of southern Arizona lived in a fairly comfortable climate. We know this because archaeologists have discovered charcoal made from hickory at the sites they occupied, and hickory grows only in a land where rainfall is plentiful. But as the Arizona climate became drier, the Cochise people had more and more difficulty in finding food. Hunger sometimes is a good means of prodding human beings into making progress, and the grinding of seeds was an early Cochise response to the need for new sources of food. Later came the discovery of corn.

Corn is a remarkable vegetable. It resists almost every extreme of climate and produces a generous yield of nutritious food. Corn can grow under near-desert conditions and in the rain-flooded fields of India. It does well as far north as Canada and Russia, as far south as the tropics. It grows below sea level in eastern Europe, and at heights of 12,000 feet in the Peruvian Andes. There are hundreds of different varieties of corn, adapted to many types of growing conditions.

In the Americas, the cultivation of corn probably began in Peru or Mexico, seven or eight thousand years ago. The

Indians of those countries were always more advanced than their cousins to the north. But one of the earliest places where corn was grown was New Mexico. At Bat Cave, in western New Mexico, archaeologists found small corncobs buried in a layer of debris that also included weapon points in the Cochise style. Carbon-14 analysis of the cobs gave an age of nearly six thousand years. The corn was extremely primitive, each ear only a few inches long and lacking a husk. But the Bat Cave corncobs indicate that the Cochise folk had learned the secrets of agriculture by 4000 B.C.

It was a giant step. Now they no longer depended entirely on luck in foraging, and as a result the Cochise culture began to grow more complex. People who have to spend all their time digging and scratching for food do not have the leisure to develop new ways of doing things. Progress requires thinking, and thinking is not easy when the whole day is passed in the struggle to find enough food to keep alive.

The rate of progress speeds up once a steady food supply is assured. The Cochise people, becoming more efficient farmers all the time, began to improve their entire way of life now that they had the bounty of corn. They could live all winter on corn stored the summer before, and that gave them time to think. By about 1000 B.C. the Cochise people had a fairly advanced agricultural society. They were the first true farmers in North America. Occupying much of southern Arizona and New Mexico, they lived in small villages near their fields. They learned the arts of basketry, using the tough fibers of such desert plants as the yucca. They made sandals and mats and nets for themselves. They dug shallow pits for houses, roofing them over with twigs and small branches.

About 300 B.C., the farmers of Arizona learned how to make pottery. This was something that probably came to them from the Indians of Mexico. Water-tight vessels of clay allowed the Cochise people to make another big jump forward. Now they could cook their food more easily, boiling things in sturdy pots; now they could carry water from great distances; now they could store surplus corn in safety.

There were so many changes in Cochise society, now that it had pottery, that archaeologists do not use the term "Cochise" to describe this more advanced culture. Instead they consider the Cochise to have divided into two daughter-cultures, which they call the Hohokam and the Mogollon.

The earlier of these two new traditions is the Mogollon, which is thought to have established an independent existence about 200 or 300 B.C. The Mogollon people grew out of the Cochise without any marked break; they simply were better at farming and homebuilding, and they could make pottery.

The Mogollon folk have only been known to archaeologists since 1930, when the first evidence of their settlements was discovered. They were named after the Mogollon Mountains of southeastern Arizona and New Mexico, which themselves were named for an eighteenth-century Spanish governor, Don Juan de Mogollon. (The name is locally pronounced MUG-ey-on.)

The Mogollon country is high and dry; the hills are covered with the scrubby underbrush common to arid mountainsides. It was never an easy place for farmers to thrive. The Mogollon raised their crops in the mountain valleys, made simple pottery that gradually improved, and built fairly extensive villages.

Archaeologists have identified a number of separate stages of Mogollon culture between 300 B.C. and 1100 A.D., when they came in contact with other civilizations and were absorbed. In the earliest, or Pine Lawn, phase, the Mogollon folk lived in pits two to five feet deep, with an entrance ramp on one side. The walls were of plain earth; the roofs were logs covered with a layer of small branches, and with a coating of mud plaster to hold everything in place. Small pits were dug in the floors of these pit-houses to serve as storage bins and as fireplaces. The bigger Mogollon villages consisted of twenty or thirty of these pit-houses. Some villages had larger pits also, which may have been used for religious purposes.

The Mogollon pottery of this time was brown or red in color, otherwise undecorated. The Mogollon people made stone pipes for smoking tobacco, and fashioned manos and metates, mortars and pestles, hammers, spear points, and other tools from stone. About the time of Christ they developed the bow and arrow, which came to replace the thrown spear as the chief Mogollon weapon.

The changes in Mogollon culture over the centuries were gradual but steady. In the second stage, the Georgetown phase (500–700 A.D.), Mogollon potters began to paint broad geometric designs in red on their brown pottery—a trivial change to us, but one that may have seemed revolutionary in the Mogollon villages. The pit-houses grew deeper and bigger, and all were equipped

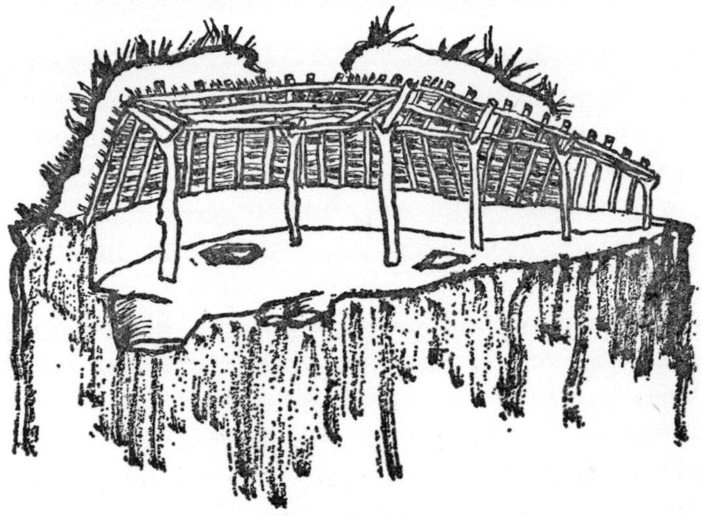

Pit house, side view

now with fire-pits. In the next stage, the San Francisco (700–900 A.D.)—named for a river that flows through western New Mexico—the shape of Mogollon pit-houses changed from circular to rectangular. Now the Mogollon dwellings were five or six feet deep, ten feet wide and twelve feet long, with an entrance ramp sloping up from the floor to the ground level outside. A central post supported the roof of logs and brush covered with mud plaster. There were further changes in pottery design, significant to archaeologists because they make it easier to determine the age of a given Mogollon site. The red-on-brown decorations became thinner, more refined; then a style of red-on-white pottery became popular, and, much later, black-on-white.

While the Mogollon culture was developing in the mountains, another offshoot of the Cochise people began to establish itself to the west, in the Arizona desert.

These folk were the Hohokam—so named by the archaeologist Harold S. Gladwin in the late 1920's, when he began to carry out research in the Gila River section of Arizona. The term is one used by the modern Pima Indians of Arizona for the early inhabitants of their region, and means "ancient people," or "those who have gone away."

The Hohokam lived in dry country. Mesquite and cactus were the typical vegetation of their area. The rainfall seldom amounted to more than ten inches during the year, and in the summer the temperature was over 100° much of the time. The Hohokam raised corn, squash, beans, and later cotton, in this desert. There was only one way farmers could survive there: they had to build a canal system that would bring water from the rivers to their fields.

Like the Mogollon, the Hohokam lived in pit-houses, but the design was somewhat different. Typical Hohokam dwellings of the earliest period were square or rectangular. The pits were about two or three feet deep, and as big as 32 feet square. The walls and roofs were of cottonwood or mesquite beams, over which a matting of twigs, reeds, grass, and earth was laid. As with the Mogollon, the design of these houses slowly evolved over the centuries. At any one time, everyone built his house to look pretty much like those of his neighbors, but the styles did change as time passed.

About 500 A.D., the Hohokam added to their villages a new and unusual feature: ball-courts. These were flat, oval areas, as much as 200 feet long and 60 feet wide, with earthen embankments along the borders. We are in a position to make a good guess as to how these courts were used, because they look very much like similar courts built by the Maya Indians in Mexico and Central America. Spanish chroniclers watched the Maya games and left accounts of them.

The idea of the game, apparently, was to pass a solid ball of rubber through hoops mounted at the ends of the arena. The basic theory was something like modern basketball, but the action was closer to that of soccer, since the players could not touch the ball with the hands, and had to knock or butt the ball through the goal. This game evidently was more than simply a sport for the Maya, and had some religious significance unknown to us today.

Since the Indians of Central America fifteen centuries ago were far more advanced than those of Arizona, it is reasonable to think that the ball-court notion originated among the Maya and was adopted, for some reason, by the Hohokam. The presence of these courts in the Hohokam villages is one of the best indications of contact between the early inhabitants of the Southwest and those of Central America. Perhaps traveling merchants from the Maya country passed through Hohokam land and told the natives about the game. Small copper bells made in Mexico have been found in Hohokam sites, indicating that such trade did exist.

There were other Indian groups living in southern Arizona and New Mexico during the Hohokam-Mogollon era, but their cultures are not nearly so well known. The Hohokam and Mogollon were the heirs of the Cochise, who were the first farmers of the Southwest. They were the most advanced Indians in North America of their time.

But the Hohokam and Mogollon were destined to be outdistanced by neighbors to the north. The people of the north were slower starters, and were still gathering nuts when the Hohokam and Mogollon were harvesting corn. But they learned swiftly, perhaps absorbing some ideas from the farmers of the south. The civilization that they built developed into the most interesting and most elaborate in all of North America.

THE PEOPLE OF THE FOUR CORNERS

On a high plateau in the southwestern United States is the only point in our country where four states meet. Arizona, New Mexico, Colorado, and Utah come together at right angles, and so the general area around the meeting-place is called the "Four Corners" country.

There is something a little arrogant about that nickname, because the boundary lines creating those corners were drawn only a few generations ago. Long before there were any states, any boundaries, or any invisible "corners" on that plateau, it was Indian country. The civilization of the Pueblos was born there, fifteen or twenty centuries ago.

It is spectacularly beautiful country. Though geologists call the region a plateau, it is anything but monotonously flat; there are prairies, mountains, deep gorges, eroded terraces, steeply-rising mesas. Cliffs of bright red sandstone sparkle in the hard, clear sunlight. It is dry country, but not nearly so dry as the desert land where the Hohokam once lived, and not nearly so hot. Even at the height of summer the daytime temperatures are comfortable. At night there can be a sharp chill even in July, because of the altitude, much of the area being more than 10,000 feet above sea level. Where the land is high, it is covered with a forest of stumpy pinyon pines and gnarled junipers; in the lowlands, the gray-green sagebrush spreads over mile after mile, dotted with clumps of yucca and beargrass.

Rivers crisscross the plateau. The Rio Grande runs roughly north-south through central New Mexico; the San Juan traces an east-west course through southern Utah and the Colorado-New Mexico border country; the vast Colorado River curves boldly through Colorado, Utah, and Arizona. These rivers have carved canyons over the millennia, tirelessly slashing away at the sandstone through which they flow. Of these, the Grand Canyon of the Colorado is the best known and the biggest, but there are many others, some of them of great importance in the story of Indian life. The rivers that cut these mighty canyons are not very mighty themselves, except for a few. Most are shallow and muddy through much of the year, coming to life only when spring thaws pump torrents into their beds. In the summer many of the rivers and streams are completely dry. The site of such a river, dry except for brief periods during the year, is called a *wash.* Sometimes a heavy summer rain sends a flash flood racing through a wash, cutting the channel a little deeper, helping to create a canyon of tomorrow.

Not many people live in the Four Corners country. There are some towns, fast growing into small cities—Durango, Colorado; Farmington, New Mexico; Holbrook, Arizona. But much of the land is empty. The entire northeast corner of Arizona belongs to the Navaho and Hopi Indians, and though the Navaho are numerous as Indian tribes go, there are only some ninety thousand of them living on a reservation bigger than many eastern states. The visitor can travel fifty miles at a stretch without seeing a single sign of human existence, except for an occasional isolated Navaho trading post.

Only in July and August does the Four Corners country seem at all crowded. That is tourist time, when thousands of sightseers arrive. There is much to see: the stunning cleft that is the Grand Canyon, the many-hued beauty of the Painted Desert, the fantasy-world of the Petrified Forest, the soaring arch of Rainbow Bridge. Those are the natural features, and they stagger the mind and daze the imagination. People come, also, to see the remaining Indians, to buy a Navaho rug or a Hopi bowl.

And everywhere, not always apparent to the casual eye, are the relics of a bygone age. Some are as spectacular in their way as the Grand Canyon: the cliff houses of Mesa Verde and Kayenta, the monumental dead cities of Pueblo Bonito, the great dwelling that bears the misleading name of Aztec Ruins. Other tokens of the past are more elusive: a low mound with bits of broken pottery scattered over its surface, or a patch of earth a little looser and softer than its surrounding soil.

Here the Pueblo story began. An ingenious, stubborn, doggedly determined band of farmers came to dwell here, and left their mark. They started by living in caves and shallow pits, and eventually built the grandest cities on the continent. They are the direct ancestors of the pueblo-dwellers encountered by Coronado and Espejo and Oñate. They are the forebears of the Indians of the twenty-five surviving pueblos of the twentieth century.

Archaeologists often call these unusual folk the Anasazi. It is a word from the language of the Navaho, who are Indians that came to the Southwest fairly late themselves. It means "the Old Ones"—the builders of the great ruins of the Four Corners country. Two main divisions of the Anasazi civilization are recognized: the early stage, called the Basketmaker phase, and the later or Pueblo phase.

The Basketmakers came to the Four Corners country about two thousand years ago. We know very little about their earlier life. Possibly they were desert-dwellers from Utah or Nevada; perhaps they drifted up from Cochise country in the south. They wandered into the Four Corners region in small groups, a few families at a time. There they found what seemed to them like a friendly environment. They had just enough water to allow them to raise their corn and squash, and along the steep canyon walls there were shallow caves in which they could take shelter.

Their culture was a simple one in its early days. They could farm, more or less; they had heard how the people of the south planted seeds and watered the ground and made crops grow, and they imitated them, clumsily at first. Small cornfields provided enough food for survival. The caves that were their homes were hardly more than niches, open to the sun and the wind. Where no caves were handy, they built crude shelters of brush.

The Basketmakers were not very good farmers at the start. They had not yet learned the tricks of coaxing the soil to yield its bounty, and they had to add to their food supply by gathering fruits and seeds in the valleys. They dug storage pits in the sandy floors of their caves to hold the nuts, berries, and seeds that they collected. These pits were two or three feet deep and four or five feet across, with floors that were sometimes covered with slabs of sandstone or a coating of mud, and sides that were often lined with stone. Mud plastering sealed up the chinks between the stone slabs to keep vermin out. Protection was also provided by covering the storage pits with round sandstone slabs, or with roofs made of small poles plastered with mud.

The knack of making pottery had not yet found its way north from the Mogollon and Hohokam regions. The Basketmakers relied instead on the basketwork that gave them their modern name. They made baskets in great numbers and used them for a wide variety of purposes.

Basketwork was identified as the "trademark" of the earliest Anasazi as far back as 1893. In that year a man named Richard Wetherill discovered ninety bodies in a cave near Grand Gulch, Utah, and with them were many finely woven baskets. Wetherill, who was a major figure in the archaeological rediscovery of the Anasazi, was more a cowboy than an archaeologist, but he was shrewd and surprisingly scientific in his work. A decade earlier he had found the remarkable cliff houses of Mesa Verde. Now, carefully cleaning out the cave, he observed that the artifacts of these basketmaking people seemed more primitive than those of the more familiar Anasazi, and he concluded that these people, whom he named the Basketmakers, had lived earlier than the builders of the cliff houses and had had a different kind of culture. Modern archaeology has shown that his guess was correct.

We can reconstruct Basketmaker life down to many of its smallest details, thanks to the dry climate that preserved so much for the archaeologists to find. We know that the Basketmakers were not very different physically from the Pueblo Indians of today. They were short and stocky, with light brown skins and coarse black hair. They wore little clothing, perhaps just a scrap of cloth around the waist. During the winter, and on the colder evenings, they may have worn robes made of strips of rabbit fur tied together with yucca fibers. They buried their dead in such robes, and it seems likely that they wore similar robes in life.

One item of clothing that was universal in the Basketmaker world was the sandal. The Four Corners country is rough and rocky, with an abundance of spiny, thorny plants; not even the stoic Indians care to walk around barefoot there. The Basketmakers wove sandals out of the fibers of the yucca plant and the apocynum, a plant

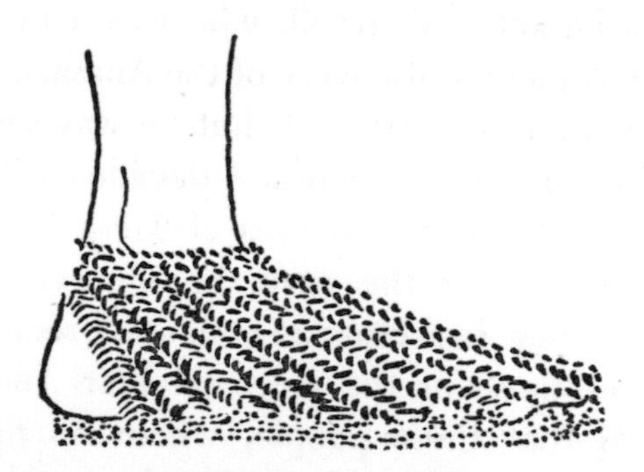

Basketmaker sandal

related to the milkweed. They were thick-soled and square-toed, and often were decorated with a toe fringe of buckskin or shredded juniper bark. A cord, frequently made of twined human hair, was passed through loops at the heel and toe of the sandal and around the wearer's ankle, to hold the footgear in place. Archaeologists have found several pairs of Basketmaker sandals coated with mud, as though they had been used as galoshes in bad weather.

Yucca fibers served also as the raw material for baskets. Basketmakers deftly wove this tough substance into trays and bowls, which often were handsomely decorated with symmetrical patterns. They constructed their large wide-mouthed baskets by building up coil after coil of small willow rods padded with yucca fiber, each coil being attached to the one below it with a thin willow splint that passed through holes punched by awls made of bone. Decorations were produced by using splints that had been dyed black or red.

The baskets had many uses. Some, coiled so closely as to be watertight, were used for cooking; and because the Basketmakers did not yet have pottery, they resorted to a roundabout method of cooking that many primitive people employ. They could not set their fiber baskets over fires, so they filled them with water and dropped red-hot stones into them until the water boiled. In this way they could cook stews and soups.

Other baskets were used for carrying water from far-away springs or rain pools. These had narrower mouths than the cooking baskets, to keep water from splashing out. Often they were coated inside with pine resin to make them watertight. Loops made of human hair were fastened to them for carrying.

Hair was an important and useful material for the Basketmakers. It was twined into ropes and belts, and used for fashioning hunting nets. A remarkable Basketmaker net found at White Dog Cave near Kayenta, Arizona, contained some four miles of string. It was two hundred and forty feet long, more than three feet wide, and weighed twenty-eight pounds. Such nets, looking very much like tennis nets, were probably strung across the mouths of narrow gorges and canyons, and small animals were stampeded into them and were killed. Two sections of the White Dog Cave net were made of a mixture of hair and apocynum fiber, giving them a darker appearance than the rest of the net. Possibly this was done to create the illusion of an opening toward which the frightened animals might rush.

The hair for these elaborate nets was contributed by the Basketmaker women. They hacked off hanks of their hair whenever they needed weaving material, using crude stone knives. We know this because several well-preserved "mummies" of Basketmakers have been found in caves in the Four Corners region. (These are not true mummies, since they were not chemically embalmed as the Egyptians treated their dead. Rather, they were naturally preserved by the dry Southwestern climate and the absence of decay bacteria.) Such Basketmaker "mummies" show the women's hair cropped to a length of two or three inches.

Basketmaker men, on the other hand, evidently preferred a more elegant coiffure. They wore their hair long, sometimes binding it into three tresses, one on each side and one in back. In a few cases male Basketmakers have been found with a part carefully clipped out from forehead to crown, and a cord-bound pigtail in back. This fancier hair style may have indicated high rank or have had some special religious significance. Hairbrushes of yucca fiber have been found at Basketmaker sites.

To make themselves look even more decorative by contrast with their short-haired womenfolk, Basketmaker men were fond of wearing ornaments in their hair. They tied bone points together to make comb-like trinkets that were topped with feathers. Basketmakers of both sexes wore necklaces, bracelets, and ear pendants. Some of these were of polished stone, some of bone, and some were made of the shells of sea creatures such as olivella and abalone. The presence of such shells in Basketmaker dwellings indicates that there must have been trade routes linking the Four Corners with the Pacific coastal region.

Since the Basketmakers had time to think about hairdos and jewelry, they obviously were growing more skilled as farmers. At first, perhaps, they simply dumped seed in the ground and left it to sprout by itself. But over the centuries they learned how to tend their crops, how to water them and protect them from marauding animals, how to harvest them properly and store food through the winter months. The gradual improvement in farming techniques freed more and more of the Basketmakers for such nonessential tasks as making jewelry and decorated baskets.

Corn was their most important crop. They planted their

fields in the canyon bottoms below their hillside shelters, using hardwood digging-sticks about four feet long to get the seed into the ground. The corn was planted at a depth of a foot or more, to take advantage of underground moisture. When they were lucky enough to grow a surplus of corn, they stored the extra ears in their underground storage pits for a winter food supply. Squash was another important food crop, and the hollowed-out gourds served as vessels. Then, too, they varied their diets with roots, bulbs, grass seeds, sunflower seeds, pinyon nuts, and other wild foods. We know this because caches of such roots and seeds and nuts have been found at Basketmaker sites. Apparently the Basketmakers also made use of the edible fruit of certain cacti; no supplies of stored cactus fruit have ever been found, but a shrewd archaeologist once detected a cactus seed wedged in the tooth of a Basketmaker jaw!

For their meat supply, the Basketmakers snared or netted gophers, badgers, rabbits, prairie dogs, and other small animals. Deer, mountain lion, bears, and mountain sheep were also hunted, and were slain with spears propelled by cleverly designed throwing sticks. The throwing stick—known by its Aztec name of *atlatl*—was about two feet long, two inches wide, and half an inch thick. A spear or dart was fitted, butt-end first, into a prong at one end of the atlatl. The hunter grasped the throwing stick by two finger-loops near the middle, drew his arm back and threw. Use of the stick gave him greater wrist-power and sent the spear forward at higher speed.

The Basketmakers did not begin to use bows and arrows for many centuries, although they were in use among the Hohokam and Mogollon to the south. They were never a warlike people, but they occasionally came in conflict with their neighbors, and the spear must have seemed a clumsy weapon indeed in competition with the bow. In Canyon del Muerto, Arizona, evidence of a massacre of Basketmakers was found, showing how some roving tribe equipped with bows and arrows had wiped out a band of peaceful farmers.

Such encounters probably were rare in the sparsely-settled Four Corners country. Life was peaceful and quiet among the Basketmakers most of the time. They went through their yearly round, the men working in the fields or hunting, the women skillfully weaving baskets and nets. It was no longer necessary to spend all the time collecting food. During the long winter months, stored supplies carried the tribe along, and there was leisure to develop new ways of thought, new ways of life.

The Basketmakers began to ponder the problem of life after death. They wondered, as all human beings do, whether there was some existence after this one. Did a man go out like a snuffed candle after the thirty or forty years of his life, or was there some other world where the dead lived again?

Like all other American Indians, the Basketmakers had no knowledge of writing. They left us no books of theology, no scriptures, no record of their religious beliefs. Yet we can be fairly certain that they gave thought to these matters, and that they came to believe in a life after death.

Basketmaker sites have yielded rattles made of deer hoofs and bone, which probably were used in religious ceremonies. Whistles of hollow bird bones may also have been employed in Basketmaker rituals. On cliff faces are found images, painted or cut in the rock, that could well have had spiritual meaning. These designs (called *petroglyphs* if they are cut into the rock and *pictographs* if they are painted on it) show lizards, birds, human figures, hands, and such abstract forms as whorls, loops, and zigzags. They are found wherever ancient men lived in the Southwest.

More revealing still are Basketmaker burials. The early Basketmakers dug storage pits for food, and after a while they began to use similar pits as graves. They buried their dead in a flexed position, with the knees drawn up almost to the chin. The bodies were tenderly wrapped in blankets of rabbit fur, or placed in large woven bags. Into each burial pit went personal possessions of the departed one, as though the Basketmakers believed he would need them in the life to come.

Food, weapons, baskets, nets, beads, ornaments, digging-sticks, stone pipes—all these have been uncovered in Basketmaker graves. With nearly every burial is found a pair of new unworn sandals, the clearest sign that the Basketmakers expected their dead to enter another world where a fresh pair of sandals would be useful.

Often there were group burials. Two, three, or four Basketmakers might be laid to rest in the same pit. One grave contained nineteen closely-packed bodies, indicating that the village may have suffered some devastating epidemic. The burial pits were usually lined with bark, grass, or fiber, and the bodies covered with the same materials; slabs of stone, poles, brush, and dirt were laid down as covers for the tombs.

There are some extremely strange Basketmaker burials. An Arizona pit yielded the body of a man in leather moccasins, an item rarely found among the sandal-wearing Basketmakers. His body had been cut in two at the waist, apparently after death, and then sewed together again. Was he a stranger from some far tribe who had met death in Basketmaker country? And had the Basketmakers, curious to see if such moccasin-wearing men were really human, opened his corpse for a close inspection?

Equally puzzling is a burial from the Canyon del Muerto, in northeastern Arizona. The pit contained only a pair of arms and hands, lying palms up on a bed of grass. Three handsome necklaces of abalone shell were wrapped around the wrists, and two pairs of magnificent sandals were included in the grave offerings. A large basket lay over the remains. Was this the last resting place of some bold one who had met a terrible death? Perhaps the rest of his body had been destroyed as he perished, and his people, finding only his arms, had buried them lovingly and with full ceremony.

The early Basketmaker burials were in pits dug in cave floors. As time passed there came to be little room available in the caves for further burials, and the Basketmakers began to dig their burial pits in the open, or along hillsides below their caves. Soon they started to abandon the caves even as places to live in. They moved to open ground and began to build small villages.

This movement became general about 450 or 500 A.D. It marks the beginning of what archaeologists call the Modified Basketmaker period. That does not mean that anything like a revolution spread through Basketmaker country. Nor was there a specific moment when all the

Basketmakers convened and declared, "It is time for us to become Modified Basketmakers." Rather, it was an extremely gradual process. Some Basketmaker tribes were centuries ahead of others in adopting the new ways.

The forerunners of the new phase may have lived in the valley of the Animas River, north of Durango, Colorado. The earliest known Basketmaker village was found there in 1938 and 1939 by the archaeologist Earl H. Morris. The tree-ring method of dating has since shown that it was occupied between 46 and 330 A.D.

There were about fifty houses, some built on a sloping hillside, others on a man-made terrace. They were roughly circular pits, ranging from thirty feet across to a third of that diameter. The floors were covered with a clay coating that curved upward to meet the half-buried logs forming the walls. Above these wall foundations, horizontally-stacked timbers, set in mud, rose and sloped inward, and a roofing layer of logs, brush, and mud covered the top of the walls to form a dome. Inside there were storage pits sunk in the floor, fireplaces, and a pit to hold the manos and metates. There was probably a smoke-hole in the roof, and perhaps this also served as the entrance to the pit-house. The roof was just high enough to allow a man to stand upright—which is to say that it was barely five feet high, since the Basketmakers were short people.

The pit-house idea did not seem to be popular. This village in Colorado eventually was abandoned, and more than a century and a half went by before the notion of building such colonies became widespread. The earliest house of the real Modified Basketmaker period has been dated 475 A.D.

Probably most of the Basketmakers were living in pit-house villages by 550 or 600. The heart of their territory was still the Four Corners country, particularly along the valley of the San Juan River, but Modified Basketmaker remains have been found as far west as Nevada, as far east in New Mexico as Santa Fe, and as far south as the region beyond Zuni Pueblo.

The villages varied. Some had only a few houses, others as many as a hundred. The earliest pit-houses were round, but in time the most widely-used design was oval, and still later a rectangular or square form with rounded corners was adopted. The pits were two to five feet deep, nine to thirty feet across. Some were plastered with mud; more usually their walls were lined with slabs of stone, or a combination of slabs and plaster was used.

The pits were roughly dome-shaped, with sturdy roofs made of timber and reeds plastered with mud. An entrance passageway was left open in the side wall. A second opening, in the roof, permitted smoke to escape from the fireplace on the floor below. After a while the Basketmakers began to use this hatchway in the roof as their entrance. They would descend into the house on a ladder thrust through the opening. The old entrance passageways were kept to provide ventilation for the fires, but were greatly reduced in size.

It is not hard to see that there could be difficulties in entering a pit-house through the smoke-hole while a fire was burning. A sudden gust of wind whipping through the ventilator opening could fan the cooking fire into a blazing flare. To prevent this, the Basketmakers mounted an upright slab of stone between the ventilator opening and the fire-pit. Such a slab, known as a *deflector,* kept the inrushing air from stirring up a blaze or putting the fire out altogether.

The floor of the pit-house was smoothly plastered with clay or paved with slabs of stone. The fire-pit was in the center of the room. Storage-pits were dug in the floor of the house at first, but afterwards separate storage-pits were grouped around the dwelling-place. Some of the bigger pit-houses were actually two-room structures, with a storage area attached to the living-quarters.

The houses had little furniture. Chairs and beds were unknown. The family slept on blankets and crouched on the floor to eat. The household utensils—manos, metates, baskets, storage bags, and, later, pots and jugs—were kept in niches along the wall. The Basketmakers probably spent little time in their houses, since the dark, smoky, low-roofed pits were hardly comfortable. They lived and worked outdoors, entering the houses only to sleep or to take shelter against bad weather. By the middle of the Modified Basketmaker period, the usual design of the pit-house showed a flat-topped roof instead of a domed one, and much of the household activity took place on the roof, which became an open-air living area for the family.

One other feature of the pit-house deserves mention. Nearly every house had a small circular hole in its floor, on the side of the fire-pit opposite the deflector. This hole was usually filled with clean sand. If the people of the Four Corners had died out without leaving descendants, we might never have known the purpose or meaning of that small hole. But it happens that Pueblo Indians of today still build a kind of pit-house, not as a dwelling but as a ceremonial hall, the kiva. Kivas have small floor-holes just where they are found in the pit-houses of Modified Basketmakers. The Pueblos believe that such a hole, known as a *sipapu,* represents the place where their ancestors first emerged into this world from the underworld where they were created. It seems very likely that this myth goes back at least fifteen centuries to Modified Basketmaker days, and that the sipapus of today have their counterparts in the shallow depressions found in ancient pit-house floors.

The pit-houses were grouped in small clusters. In time the villages grew bigger, so that some may have had populations of several hundred. Though some Basketmakers had moved out into the valleys, others continued to live in the shallow caves along cliff walls, building their pit-houses in the floors of the caves. The valley-dwellers made steady and relatively rapid progress, and their houses grew bigger and sturdier. Perhaps about 700 A.D., they started to build certain houses, standing apart from the rest of the village and presumably used for religious or ceremonial purposes. These were in the pit-house style, but much bigger, and possibly an entire village might have crowded into them to take part in community rituals.

This development of architecture and of more complex religious practices was made possible by advances in Basketmaker agriculture. New varieties of corn were grown, with bigger ears than the earlier kinds. The cultivation of beans was another great forward step. Beans, a high-protein food, enhanced the Indian diet considerably. But whereas corn requires fairly little attention during the growing season, beans must be cultivated with diligence. The fact that the Modified Basketmakers grew them shows how much they had learned about farming in the six or seven centuries since their arrival in the Four Corners country.

Hunting was made easier by the adoption of the bow and arrow. Two new stone tools appeared: the hammer and the axe. Before this, timbers for house construction had been shaped by burning the wood.

Pottery now appeared in the Basketmaker villages. It was crude stuff. The Hohokam and Mogollon had been expert potters for centuries, but somehow the technique did not reach the Basketmakers until the sixth or seventh century. The first Basketmaker use of the rich clay of their region came about 300 A.D., when they started to make dishes and vessels of dried mud. Possibly some Basketmaker woman lined a water-basket with clay, and noticed how the clay hardened when left to dry in the sun. She went on to experiment with vessels made out of clay alone, thinking that it would be simpler to press clay into the shape of a pot than to weave an elaborate basket.

When left in the sun, the clay hardened, but it was brittle and cracked easily. The next step was to temper the clay: that is, to add something to bind it together. Shredded juniper bark was one of the first tempering materials used. But these thick clumsy bowls were still likely to fall apart when handled, or to melt into shapelessness when used as water jars or cooking pots. The introduction of sand as a tempering material made the vessels a little more durable, but still not sturdy enough.

Then someone may have brought back word from

Mogollon country that the clay pots would last longer if they were dried in a hot fire. The Basketmaker women tried it, building little mounds of firewood around their newly made vessels. Sometimes the pots cracked in the fire. Those that did not emerged strong and waterproof. They were excellent for storing seeds, for carrying water, for cooking food.

By 600 A.D. Basketmaker pottery techniques were showing rapid improvement. The women brought clay from favorite quarries and rolled it into thick ropelike coils. They placed one coil of clay atop another until they had built up a pot in the shape they desired. For temper they used sand, crushed rock, or the powdered sherds of vessels that had cracked during firing. After they had joined the coils, they would make the walls of the pot smooth by scraping them with a piece of wood or a bit of broken pottery. Then they would place them in the fire.

The first Basketmaker pottery was white or dull gray in color. It was produced by firing the vessels in a partly smothered fire poorly supplied with oxygen. The Mogollon had discovered that their pottery could be given a handsome red, brown, or yellow color by letting air circulate freely through the fire, but this technique did not reach the northern Indians for many years.

Some of the more enterprising Basketmaker potters began to decorate their ware. One favorite decoration was a row of bands on the neck of a pot, produced by leaving the original rings of clay unscraped on the neck, while rubbing the rest of the vessel smooth. These neck-banded pots were usually gray. Simple designs were painted on the white vessels. The potters used a vegetable paint, probably made by boiling the juice of a plant called bee-weed. The brushes were yucca leaves whose ends had been chewed until the fibers softened and split. The decorations consisted of geometrical forms, lines and squiggles and dots. Sometimes crudely-drawn animal images were painted on the pottery.

Jars, bowls, dishes, ladles, storage jugs—the Anasazi women had a whole array of new vessels. But they kept on making baskets, and in fact their artistry in weaving grew even greater, though many types of baskets disappeared after pottery became common. Sandals, however, could not be replaced by pottery, and the craftsmen of the Modified Basketmaker period produced some superb new designs, using red, yellow, and black cord to create patterns on the upper surfaces and sometimes on the soles as well. The old square-toed type now gave way to a more graceful scallop-toed model. The beauty of these late Basketmaker sandals tells us how much these people valued artistic accomplishment. Later, when their skills had increased, they would devote the same care to their pottery as they now did to their basketry and sandals.

Their religious life grew steadily richer. We can only guess, of course, at the beliefs they held. But archaeologists have found a wealth of ceremonial objects in the later Basketmaker villages. There are odd clay figurines in human shape, a few inches long; corncobs decorated with sticks or feathers; polished stone disks; "medicine bags" containing all manner of small objects of probable sacred significance; tapered stone cylinders used as tobacco pipes. The Anasazi must have spent long hours developing and expanding their religious beliefs. Probably they divided themselves into clans, organized prayer societies, held complex ritual observances.

The beginnings of the Pueblo culture sprang from those pit-houses of the sixth and seventh and eighth centuries. But the pit-houses themselves no longer answered to Anasazi needs. A time came when men wearied of living underground. The pioneers of a new school of architecture began to build houses of a different kind, and an era ended. The first pueblos appeared.

THE EARLY PUEBLOS

ARCHAEOLOGY IS A kind of detective work. The clues lie buried in the earth; the archaeologist uncovers them with the greatest care, studies them, draws his conclusions. From bits of pottery and the crumbling foundations of ruined buildings he tries to reconstruct an entire civilization, its thoughts and dreams, its art and culture, its birth, growth, and decay.

Like detectives, archaeologists sometimes make mistakes, as any archaeologist will freely admit. The evidence is not always clear. Clues can be misread. False interpretations can deceive a whole generation of scholars. What seems obvious is not so obvious after all, and later evidence can upset a widely-accepted theory.

That is exactly what happened in the Southwest. Beginning in the 1890's, the ancient ruins of the Basketmakers were discovered in great numbers. The people, as we have seen, lived in pit-houses, had little or no knowledge of pottery, seem not to have used bows and arrows through most of their existence, and were relatively backward as farmers. The "mummies" and skeletons found associated with the Basketmaker artifacts indicate that they had been people with long, narrow skulls.

At the same time, Indian ruins of a different sort were being excavated in the same regions. They yielded the remains of people whose heads had been broad and round. These round-headed Indians had lived in above-ground dwellings, had been excellent potters and skilled farmers, and had used the bow and arrow. They had obviously come to the Four Corners country later than the long-skulled Basketmakers, because many of the houses of these round-headed people were built right on top of Basketmaker sites, while there was never a Basketmaker site built on top of the other sort.

A convincing theory emerged. It held that a group of broad-headed people had invaded the Four Corners country about 700 A.D. and had pushed the Basketmakers aside; they had taken over their fields and their villages and even their arts and crafts. Archaeologists debated the location of the original homeland of these invaders, and tried to reconstruct the era of conflict that had culminated in the overthrow of the Basketmakers.

Then new evidence came to light that demolished the whole invasion theory. Hardly any reputable archaeologist accepts the invasion idea today, though it can be found in most scientific works published before 1940.

A single cultural change accounted for the presence of broad-headed people in Anasazi country. The Basketmakers had adopted a new style of cradle. The ancient cradle had consisted of a couple of flexible sticks, bent and lashed to form an oval framework. Willow twigs were tied across this frame, and a padded covering of fur and soft juniper bark was laid over them. The baby, wrapped in a fur blanket, was snug and comfortable in this yielding cradle.

But a new style of cradle was introduced in the seventh or eighth century. Now, during all the first months of their lives, the babies were strapped into cradles designed in such a way that hard boards pressed against the backs of the infants' heads; and since the bones of a baby's skull are soft and easily deformed, the rear of the head gradually became flattened, while the sides of the skull bulged out. A child reared in such a cradle would have a round broad skull, markedly flattened in back.

Why the fashion developed is a mystery. It may have come from Central America, where such head-flattening was long practiced. The Anasazi may have adopted it because it was "the latest thing" in a sophisticated part of the world, just as people in small towns today are quick to follow the fashions of Paris or New York. At any rate, it became universal in Anasazi-land, a harmless but dramatic fad that drastically changed the skull shape of an entire people. The Anasazi continued to use the head-board generation after generation; it remained popular among the Pueblos right into our own day.

There was, then, no invasion. The round-headed Four Corners people of 900 A.D. were simply the great-great-great grandchildren of the narrow-headed Modified Basketmakers. But because they were so different culturally from their ancestors, these round-headed ones are classified as Pueblos rather than as Basketmakers.

This label was applied to them a thousand years after the fact, and, like any label, it can be changed at the whim of those who applied it. When archaeologists first began dividing the Anasazi into different cultural phases, they drew up a scheme that included such fine distinctions as "Post-Basketmaker" and "Pre-Pueblo" to cover the transition between the pit-dwellers and the apartment-house-dwellers. This became too involved, and in 1927 a conference of archaeologists, held at the ruins of Pecos Pueblo, agreed on a new terminology using Roman numbers: Basketmaker I, II, and III, followed by Pueblo I, II, III, IV, and V, to denote the stages of Anasazi development.

This system had flaws, too. What the Pecos conference called Basketmaker I was a stage that did not seem to exist at all, while the distinctions between Pueblo I and Pueblo II were so slight as to be almost meaningless. In 1935 a leading archaeologist named Frank H. H. Roberts, Jr., proposed a new system that is generally accepted today, and which we shall use here. (The Roberts system, as we shall see, has one major defect too. But that does not concern us at the moment.)

Roberts dropped Basketmaker I altogether and gave Basketmaker II and III the new names of Basketmaker and Modified Basketmaker. The hallmarks of Modified Basketmaker, as we have noted, are the movement toward pit-houses, the cultivation of beans, the development of pottery, and the employment of the bow and arrow. All these new aspects of Anasazi culture led to a period of experimentation and innovation which we, following Dr. Roberts, shall call Developmental Pueblo—the old Pueblo I and Pueblo II.

It has to be stressed that the change from one era to the next always came gradually. While one group of pioneers forged ahead, many lagged behind. Just as, in the present era of jet planes, television, and atomic bombs, there are isolated tribes still living a Stone Age existence, so too there were Anasazi at all stages of cultural development at any one time—pueblo-builders in the San Juan Valley, pit-house dwellers in outlying districts, and even a few *un*modified Basketmakers still huddling in cave shelters here and there. Slowly, as word spread of the new ways of doing things, each individual group crossed the line into the next more advanced cultural level. But by the time the last Basketmakers were beginning to live above the ground, the cleverest of the Pueblos were already starting to build their huge apartment-houses. There was never any universal and simultaneous change, nor was there a sharp break between eras.

The Anasazi of the San Juan and Animas rivers region first adopted their new type of houses about 700 A.D. They drove rows of upright poles into the ground as frames for their walls, lashing reeds or grass between the openings in the poles as a binder, and plastering thick sloshes of mud over everything. At first the walls sloped inward, and the floors were set a foot or two below ground level, so that these buildings looked not very much different from the pit-houses. Then the Anasazi began building upright walls and flat-topped roofs, and no longer depressed the floors.

In early Developmental Pueblo days, villages contained both the older and the newer types of houses. For example, a ruin at Kiatuthlana, Arizona, near the New Mexico border, shows pit-houses side by side with flat-roofed four-sided buildings of the new style, some with single rooms and others with three or four chambers. At a site in Colorado, clusters of mud-walled above-ground buildings surround a central plaza in which were pit-houses. There were many transitional forms of architecture during this time of experiment.

Pit-house villages had always been built with each house a short distance from its neighbor. The new rectangular houses could be constructed with adjoining walls. Archaeologists have found them linked in rows six to fourteen rooms long. Sometimes the rows were built in a curve; other villages had L-shaped or U-shaped layouts. These rows, which are found in ruins as old as 900 A.D., are called "unit houses" or "clan houses" by the archaeologists, who think that they may have been inhabited by related family groups.

Building materials were changing too. The Anasazi began to strengthen their walls by using slabs of sandstone along with the poles and mud. In time most of the poles vanished from the design; houses now consisted of rough stones embedded in mud, perhaps with a few widely-spaced wooden supports, and a central pole to hold up the roof. The roofs themselves were made of heavy logs laid from wall to wall, covered with smaller poles and reeds, and plastered with mud.

The first stone-and-adobe houses were mostly mud, with little stone. As time passed the builders learned how to cut and shape sandstone with hammers made of harder rock. Now they could pile slabs of stone neatly, using adobe only as the mortar instead of as the chief building material. These masonry houses were much stronger than those of poles and mud or those of mud with stone inserts. It became possible to add a second story on top of the first. Villages took the form of double-tiered rooms, arranged either in a crescent or a straight row. By 1000 A.D.

this was probably the most common village pattern among the Anasazi. These unit houses were sometimes arranged in double rows—that is, a front row and a rear one, each two stories high. There were never any staircases inside such buildings; the people who lived on the top floor had to climb ladders to the roof and enter through the opening placed there for that purpose. Since the ground-level rooms had no doors, those who lived in them had to climb to the roof also, and descend through the floors of the upper-level rooms to get to their own.

The row-shaped villages almost always ran in an east-west direction. To the south or southeast of the houses could be found one or more structures of a familiar kind: circular rooms below the level of the ground. The old pit-house was still an important part of the village scene.

But it was no longer a dwelling. Now it was purely a ceremonial building. The Anasazi had retained the ancient design, perhaps out of a sentimental fondness for the kind of homes their ancestors had lived in. Here was the smoke-hole, here was the ventilator, here the sipapu, here the deflector. But the niches around the wall, which once had held pots and baskets, now held the sacred objects of religion. The pit-house had become the kiva.

Kiva, of course, is a modern Indian word. But the pueblos of today have kivas that are much like those of 1000 A.D., except for certain changes in construction. It is fair to assume that the kivas of the Developmental Pueblo period had much the same function to the community as they do in San Ildefonso and Santo Domingo and the other pueblos of today.

Looking back at those ancient kivas from the vantage

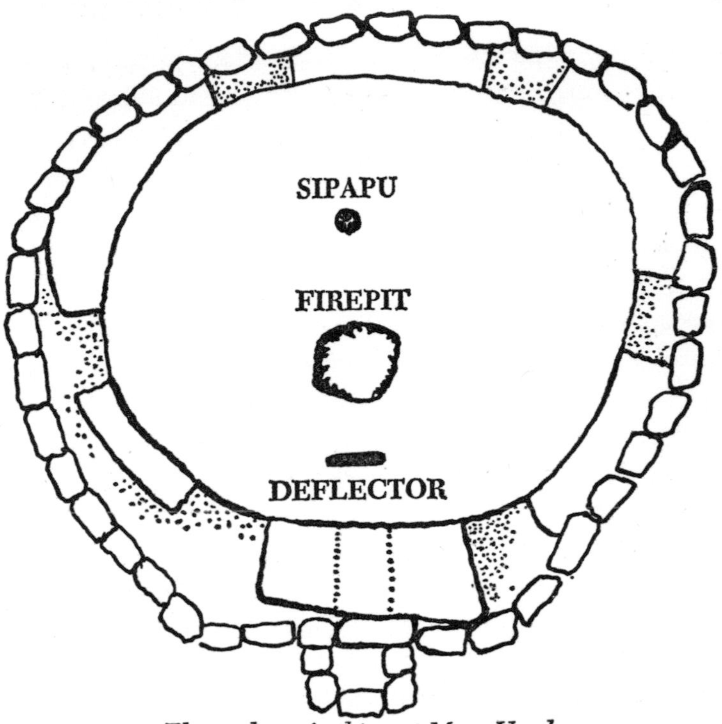

Floor plan of a kiva at Mesa Verde

point of our knowledge of modern ones, we can say that they were both religious houses and social clubs—"a combination of church and pool hall," one anthropologist has called them. In these subterranean chambers, whose roofs were flush with the ground, the most sacred religious ceremonies of the village were held. At other times the men of the village went there to talk, to relax, to exchange gossip. Women and children were allowed to enter the kiva only by special invitation, and not very often. A fire burned in the kiva much of the time, its smoke rising through the hole in the roof that was also its one entrance. On one side of the fire-pit was the sipapu, always kept carefully covered when no ceremony was in progress, so that supernatural beings could not emerge from the depths of the earth. On the other side of the fire-pit was the deflector, made of stone or of adobe brick, depending on the local fashion. Beyond the deflector was the opening of the ventilating flue, which had evolved out of the original side entrance of the pit-house. A vertical channel about a foot square ran from the floor of the kiva to the surface of the ground. The walls of the kiva were of stone, and a low stone bench circled the room. There might be six or eight stone pillars rising from this bench to a distance halfway up the wall; these were the supports for the arching vault of poles that formed the roof.

Some villages had only one kiva. Others had several. Perhaps the latter villages were divided into different clans or cult groups, each of which needed its own place of worship.

South of the kiva lay the village refuse heap. Everything useless was dumped there: broken pottery, worn-out tools, old clothing, corncobs and rabbit bones, ashes, dirt, debris. Old metates might be thrown on the heap, too, for the grinding-stones, made of soft sandstone, wore out rapidly as the energetic millers rubbed their manos against them. (The metate would simply wear through, and the particles of sandstone became mixed with the corn meal. The Indians, eating this gritty, sandy food, wore their teeth down to stubs before they reached middle age. There is still a proverb among the Pueblos: "Every man must swallow a metate during his life.")

These trash heaps are archaeological treasure troves. The discarded debris of a Pueblo village is the raw material of archaeological knowledge. Every excavation at an ancient site begins with a careful study of the village dump, which tells the archaeologists a great deal about the life of the ancient community. The Developmental Pueblo people had one custom that makes their refuse heaps particularly important to excavators: the town dump was also the town cemetery. The bodies of the dead were interred amid the debris of the village.

The Anasazi did not mean to show disrespect for the dead. The refuse heap was simply an easier place in which to dig a grave than the dry, hard-packed earth—especially in winter, when the ground might be frozen. The dead were placed in a flexed position, accompanied by offerings of pottery and other household goods. Some of the sites of the Developmental Pueblo period have just a few burials, a point which puzzles archaeologists; villages which had several hundred inhabitants for more than two hundred years yield no more than a few skeletons. Where were the rest buried? The answer remains mysterious. At some sites there is evidence that the dead were cremated. At most such evidence is lacking, and the whereabouts of the majority of the populace is unknown.

Finding Pueblo graveyards is more than a matter of ghoulish curiosity for archaeologists. Examination of the skeletons tells how the people lived. At one village the bones may show signs of malnutrition and vitamin deficiencies. At another, the great number of skeletons of children and young people may indicate some terrible epidemic. Warfare, famine, disease—the record of the graveyard can be read. Finding the body of an old woman so badly crippled that she could never have been a useful member of the community tells us something important about Anasazi civilization: in another society, that woman might have been put to death as a drag on the village, but in Anasazi-land she was allowed to live to old age, supported by the work of others. Study of skeletal remains even tells us something of marriage customs of the past. One site turned up three skeletons of people who had fused ribs. This is an unusual defect, but it can run in a family, particularly in a society where close relatives are allowed to marry and pass such traits along. Inbreeding must have been common at that pueblo.

The village pattern, then, was established by the beginning of the eleventh century. Roughly rectangular buildings made of stone mortared with mud, built side by side and more than one story high, surrounded the kiva or kivas. A refuse dump lay beyond, and the fields of corn, beans, and squash were nearby. The basic pueblo idea was born. Now the pueblos would get bigger, and then even bigger than that, until in a few centuries more they became huge structures of hundreds of rooms, many stories high.

WHILE THE ANASAZI CULTURE was growing toward greatness, the house-building idea was spreading through other civilizations of the Southwest. The Hohokam and Mogollon of the south had been skilled farmers long before the rise of the Anasazi. Now the northerners had outpaced their southern cousins, and for the first time the flow of ideas began to run from north to south.

The Mogollon people of the southern mountains had begun to change the shape of their pit-houses from circular to rectangular during the phase of their civilization that archaeologists have called the San Francisco (700–

900 A.D.). This was roughly contemporary with the shift among the Anasazi from pit-houses to rectangular above-ground dwellings. These new Mogollon houses were deeper than the older ones, and ten to twelve feet on a side. Centrally-placed poles supported the roof.

In addition, the Mogollon now began to build larger pit-houses which corresponded, it is thought, to the kivas of the Anasazi. These ceremonial houses became more common in the next phase of Mogollon development, the Three Circle period (900–1050 A.D.). They were big kidney-shaped pits, six feet deep and about 35 by 39 feet across, lined with masonry. They did not have ventilators after the Anasazi fashion, but they did have a sloping entrance passage leading to ground level. The pit-houses of this era were smaller and shallower than before, always rectangular, and generally lined with stone.

In many smaller ways the Mogollon culture seems to have been adopting Anasazi features at this time. The design of Mogollon metates shifted to imitate that of the Anasazi. Mogollon pottery came to resemble that of the northern people. It appears that waves of migrants from the Four Corners country were coming down into Mogollon territory all during the ninth, tenth, and eleventh centuries, bringing with them the exciting new developments of the north.

By the late eleventh century, the Mogollon culture had undergone so many radical changes that some archaeologists prefer to give it a new name. They call the people of the Mogollon region the *Mimbres* civilization, after the Mimbres River in whose valley the most important ruins of this culture are found. Other authorities prefer to classify the Mimbres civilization as the fifth and last phase of the Mogollon.

Whatever the label, the Mimbres folk were different in many ways from the Mogollon of previous centuries. They abandoned the slab-lined pit-houses completely, and began to build above the ground in the Pueblo manner. At first their crude rectangular houses, constructed of unshaped river boulders mortared with mud, stood separately. Then they began to link them in rows, the true pueblo layout. Mimbres pueblos had five to fifty rooms, often arranged about a court or plaza. The buildings were one story high, with floors at ground level. They had no doorways; as with the Anasazi, entrance was through the roof. The rooms were small and dark, five or six feet high and seven to twelve feet on a side. Larger rectangular rooms, partly sunk in the ground, probably served as kivas. They had ventilator shafts and fire-pits, and do not appear to have been used as living areas.

The Mimbres people customarily buried their dead beneath the floors of houses, even though the houses continued to be occupied. The bodies were buried in a flexed position deep beneath the floor, which was repaved with an adobe coating after the burial. Some Mimbres rooms had one or two burials; in one, thirty-two people had been interred. The Mimbres always included grave-offerings with their dead: metates, manos, beads, bracelets, ear pendants, hammers, pottery. Their craftsmanship was of the highest order.

Mimbres pottery is perhaps the finest ever made in the old Southwest. The usual kind of piece found in the graves was a flat, shallow bowl with a white background, on

Pottery dish, Mimbres style

which a bold design was painted in dark black. These designs often showed animals and insects—turkeys, fish, bears, deer. Many Mimbres bowls portrayed the life of the pueblo, vividly depicting men dancing, hunting, setting traps, even picking insects from corn plants. Since Mimbres painting was always clear and graphic, it provides a unique look at daily life and customs. Women are pictured wearing their hair in big looping whorls on the sides of their heads, a style still used by some Hopi girls to indicate that they are unmarried. Men are shown wearing loincloths, women wearing blankets and fringed sashes.

The Mimbres artists also decorated their bowls with

geometric figures, remarkably precise and clear. The rims of the bowls are ornamented with close-packed lines, drawn ten or fifteen to the inch without any blurring. These vigorous, attractive pieces have been found in great numbers in the Mimbres burials. Nearly every one has had a hole punched or drilled into it by its maker. This mutilation is the ceremonial "killing" of a grave offering, and was probably done at the burial to release the spirit of the bowl, enabling it to accompany the dead person on his journey to the next world. Such "killing" of grave offerings was practiced throughout the Indian world, particularly in Mexico and Central America.

The fine pottery of the Mimbres surpassed even that of the Anasazi, who were rapidly becoming superb potters themselves. Interestingly, the rediscovery of the Mimbres culture about 1914 has led to a present-day revival of Mimbres pottery. Two women of Acoma Pueblo, Lucy M. Lewis and Marie Chino, began to make bowls following the ancient Mimbres designs, although the Acoma people are Anasazi descendants and not directly linked to the Mimbres folk. Their work is as delicate and as attractive as the thousand-year-old originals, and is much sought after by collectors and museums.

The Mimbres culture seems to have reached its peak about 1200 A.D. After that the Mimbres left their valley, evidently migrating into what is now the Mexican state of Chihuahua. The Chihuahua civilization of the thirteenth and fourteenth centuries shows a combination of Anasazi and Mogollon-Mimbres traits. It had one-story houses of adobe mud reinforced with stone, and even some apartment houses three stories high. But by the time the Spaniards arrived in the middle of the sixteenth century, this Chihuahua civilization had slipped into decadence and the great adobe houses were deserted.

Swamped by ideas from the Anasazi, the Mogollon lost their individuality and were absorbed into other cultures. Their close relatives to the west, the Hohokam, also found themselves under the pressure of new ways.

The Hohokam were farmers of the desert. In the early phase of their culture—some five hundred years, beginning at the time of Christ—they depended on so-called "flood-water irrigation" for their crops; that is, they lived near streams and rivers that tended to overflow their banks during the rainy part of the year, so they planted their crops in the land moistened by the flood. This gave them a short growing season, and in a dry year there might be no flood at all, and thus no harvest.

About 500 A.D. the Hohokam began to build their first irrigation channels. By conveying water through canals from the biggest rivers to their fields, they avoided having to depend on the uncertain mercies of the rainy season. Work was slow, since their only digging tools were crude

Bowl from Acoma Pueblo, using an ancient design

wooden shovels and stone scrapers. But within two centuries the Hohokam managed to gouge out an impressive system of canals, and they went on enlarging them for hundreds of years thereafter.

It must have been an enormous community effort. Such great projects could only have been achieved after careful planning, and with the wholehearted cooperation of thousands of people. The existence of the Hohokam canals indicates a well-organized society with strong leaders.

The canals were about five feet wide and five feet deep at first, and as much as ten miles long. Through generations of patient toil under the sizzling desert sun, the canals grew bigger to meet the growing Hohokam needs. Some later canals were ten feet deep and thirty feet wide, and ran for vast distances. One system of canals in the Salt River Valley of Arizona totals 150 miles. Since the rivers carried great quantities of silt, it was necessary to work constantly at these canals, forever clearing the channels as the silt accumulated. Some of the Hohokam canals have been cleaned out in the twentieth century and incorporated into modern irrigation systems.

The Hohokam civilization was a rich and complex one. We have already seen that its people imported the mysterious ball game of the Maya about 500 A.D., building large ball courts in many villages. The Hohokam were not only clever engineers but skilled workers in stone, who fashioned excellent stone axes, grinding tools, and even jars and bowls. They lived in pit-houses. They were excellent potters long before the Anasazi mastered the techniques of working in clay. They had the bow and arrow long before the northerners, too.

The Hohokam seem to have served as busy tradesmen. Their jewelry-makers needed large quantities of the olivella and abalone shells of the Pacific, and obtained them over three trade routes leading from California across the desert regions into Arizona. They were both retailers and wholesalers; they made jewelry from the lustrous, iridescent shells and sold it to the Anasazi, and they also sold the unworked shells in quantity.

The archaeological record tells us that Hohokam traders penetrated deep into Anasazi country. Jewelry in the Hohokam style has been found at many sites in the north. The Hohokam merchants also were middlemen for goods from Mexico, such as copper bells and cotton textiles, which they took to the Anasazi. In return, the Hohokam received the produce of the Anasazi—baskets, pottery, mineral paints, and ornaments of the highly-valued blue-green stone called turquoise.

The jewelry of the Hohokam must have been in great demand. They achieved wonderful effects, making mosaics of turquoise and shell in geometric or animal-figure designs. About 1100 the Hohokam discovered the technique of etching. Perhaps they were the first people in the world to practice it, since it was not developed in Europe until the fifteenth century. The Hohokam used a mild acid, possibly made by fermenting the juice of a type of cactus, to eat designs into the backs of shells. We think they covered the shells with a coating of pitch except where they wanted the design to appear, and immersed them in acid for several days. The exposed areas were eaten away, leaving the protected part of the shell raised in relief.

During the Basketmaker era, these Hohokam tradesmen probably carried many new ideas northward along with their bundles of merchandise. The early Anasazi may have learned much about agriculture, pottery, and hunting from them. But by 800 A.D., the middle of the Developmental Pueblo period, the Anasazi were experiencing their great upsurge of growth, and soon the flow of influence was going the other way. Not only Anasazi ideas, but also the Anasazi themselves, began to enter Hohokam country. By 1300 A.D. there were many Anasazi living in the southern desert. Apparently it was a friendly invasion, for Anasazi and Hohokam shared the same towns, with their pueblos and pit-houses side by side. The old Hohokam culture began to take on many of the traits of the Anasazi.

The Anasazi themselves, by that time, were very different from the folk whom we saw building the first ramshackle unit-houses in 900 A.D. If we examine the development of Anasazi culture over the centuries, we can understand more easily why the old and distinguished Hohokam civilization was so willing to learn from the people of the north.

THE GREAT YEARS OF THE ANASAZI

THE PACE OF PROGRESS was quickening among the Anasazi. It had taken hundreds of years for them to make the move from cave shelters to pit-houses, and another three centuries had gone by before the first above-ground houses had appeared. Over the next few centuries—from 700 to 1000 A.D.—the villages grew larger, the architecture more sturdy. New ways of doing things now followed one another in swift succession.

Anasazi culture was spreading. The heart of the civilization was still the Four Corners country, particularly the San Juan Valley. There were three main centers of Anasazi life: in southwestern Colorado, the Mesa Verde area; in northwestern New Mexico, the Chaco Canyon district; and in northeastern Arizona, the vicinity of the modern town of Kayenta. In these places, similar but independent cultural groups were making rapid strides.

In outlying areas could be found less advanced groups who shared some of the Anasazi traits. In Utah, in southeastern Nevada, even as far away as the Big Bend area of Texas, Anasazi influence was felt. Some of these people still preferred to live in pit-houses; many did not have kivas; they differed from the Four Corners people in burial customs and in farming techniques. But their pottery, their household utensils, their tools and clothing, all show that they were under the sway of the vigorous, vital culture that had emerged in the Four Corners area.

There were many differences between the Anasazi of 1100 A.D. and those of 700 A.D. The most obvious, which we will turn to in a moment, was the development of the big apartment-house pueblos. Archaeologists, however, devote much attention to the changes in the style of making pottery. Open any scientific report on Southwestern archaeology and you will discover that much of the text is a discussion of minute variations in pottery techniques, illustrated with photographs of the jagged fragments of broken pots known as *potsherds*.

This emphasis on pottery often seems puzzling to laymen. Actually, pottery provides an excellent key to the development of an ancient culture. Three important factors make pottery valuable to the archaeologist. One is that at any given time, nearly everyone in an ancient culture tends to make pottery of the same general style. The second is that clay vessels are easily broken, so that a pottery-using civilization must make a great many of them. The third is that potsherds themselves are practically indestructible, and even after thousands of years of burial can be studied and classified.

Every ruined pueblo of the Southwest has thousands of potsherds scattered over its surface, and many more buried in the earth. Villagrá, who marched with Oñate in 1598, was one of the first to comment on that. "Throughout these unpeopled wastes," he wrote, "we would discover, without even taking the trouble to search, great quantities of earthenware, some in good condition, but most of it broken in pieces. It was everywhere, sometimes in heaps and sometimes scattered over the plain." Villagrá had a romantic explanation for the presence of all these sherds. The Indian kings, he said, "were very fond of this pottery, for their best utensils were of fired clay. Their tableware having once been used, [it] was forthwith broken and thrown away."

We know that nothing of the sort was done. The Indians had no kings, for one thing; and for another, the hard-working women who made the pottery would hardly stand by idly and see it smashed after a single using. The truth is that clay pots tend to break in normal wear; they are dropped or knocked over, they can crack when being heated over a fire, or they may shatter in the making. The Indians simply gathered up the pieces and dumped them on the town refuse heap, and over the centuries the accumulations of potsherds became enormous.

Tourists who visit the Southwestern ruins today are tempted to carry off potsherds as souvenirs. "There are so many of them all around," they argue. "Who would miss one or two?" But the park rangers who protect most of the ruins try to prevent this. Those potsherds are of high importance to archaeologists, who collect them, analyze them, and tally them. A survey of potsherd distribution at a given site can reveal much about the unwritten history of the Old Ones.

The first Anasazi pottery, as we have mentioned, was a plain gray or grayish-white ware, sometimes decorated

Bowl, Developmental Pueblo period

with corrugated neck-bands or with simple designs painted in vegetable paint with a yucca-fiber brush. Archaeologists finding sherds of this sort in a ruin know that they are dealing with a Modified Basketmaker or Developmental Pueblo site that was probably inhabited between 600 and 900 A.D.

There was progress in the technique of making pottery—progress which is apparent to the archaeologist studying his heaps of sherds. Preparation of the raw clay improved; first sand, then powdered rock, then ground-up potsherds were used as the tempering material. We have a good idea how the vessels were made, because the Pueblo potters of today, who are always women, now work in just about the same way as they did a thousand years ago. They never use the potter's wheel, which allows a potter to shape a vessel quickly out of a mass of clay simply by turning the clay rapidly and molding it with his hands or a tool. Instead, they build up their pots painstakingly with ring after ring of clay.

The Pueblo potter, then as now, began with a handful of wet prepared clay that had been kneaded until pliable and smooth. She would shape a saucer-like bottom for her pot. Then, usually working on an old broken pot that was used as a support, she added coil after coil of clay, turning her growing pot round and round to press each pencil-thick loop into place. The early Anasazi potters used a number of separate coils, placed one atop another, but before long they started to make their vessels from one long strand of clay coiled higher and higher. Once the pot was shaped, the potter carefully smoothed its sides, scraping and rubbing them to remove all air-bubbles, irregularities, and fingerprints. The pots then were allowed slowly to dry.

If they were intended for cooking purposes, they would not be painted, since the soot of a cooking fire would quickly obliterate any design. But vessels intended for storage, for water-carrying, or for religious uses were generally decorated. This had to be done before the pottery was fired, since vessels decorated after firing would not hold their designs.

A wash of fine light-colored clay, known as the *slip,* was applied to the surfaces of pots or bowls that were to be painted. When that had dried, the designs were painted on with yucca-fiber brushes. Finally the vessels were placed in a heap of wood and were fired to give them strength and durability.

Chaco black-on-white pottery pitcher

Most Anasazi ware was white with black designs. Other color schemes were favored in some outlying areas, as in Utah, where even in early Developmental Pueblo times the painted pottery was pinkish-orange in color, with designs in red paint. There was also black-on-red ware, and some with polished black interiors and brown or red outer walls. Producing these colors involved a careful regulation of the fire; as the Mogollon had discovered a long time before, more air was needed to yield red, yellow, or brown pottery.

Each of the important Anasazi areas had its own favorite and characteristic style of painted pottery. In the Chaco Canyon region, the pots were made with sloping sides and thin, sharp rims. The black-on-white decorations were applied with a mineral paint made from iron deposits, and took the form of many fine lines close together, triangles, interlocking rectangular patterns, checkerboards, zigzags. The designs stand out clearly and sharply from the background, perhaps because they were applied after the vessels had been given a thorough polishing.

Several hundred miles to the north, at Mesa Verde, the

painted vessels had sturdier walls than those of Chaco, with thick rims on which lines or boxes were painted. The black-on-white decorations were done with vegetable paint, and seem to fade into the surface of the vessel. Possibly they were applied before the final polishing of the unfired pot. The Mesa Verde patterns are usually geometrical, and the lines are much thicker and coarser than those of the Chaco designs.

In the Kayenta area of Arizona, the black-on-white pottery resembled that of Mesa Verde in thickness and in the use of vegetable paint. But the attractive Kayenta designs, consisting of interlocking coils and spirals and scrolls, were painted on so broadly that little of the white background shows, and at first glance the pots appear to be white-on-black rather than black-on-white. Kayenta pueblos also produced several colored styles: a black-on-orange, a black-on-red, and a polychrome pottery in red,

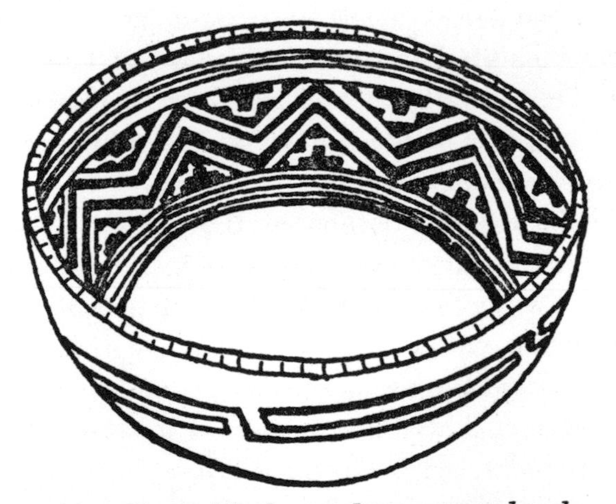

Mesa Verde black-on-white pottery bowl

black, and orange. (Pottery in more than two colors is called polychrome.)

There were other minor types of local pottery, resembling the Chaco, Mesa Verde, or Kayenta types but varying in some slight degree. These have been classified by archaeologists according to the place where they were first discovered; a technical archaeological report may refer to such types as Escavada Black-on-white, Gallup Black-on-white, McElmo Black-on-white, St. John's Polychrome, Puerco Black-on-red, and so on. Very often half a dozen varieties of potsherd are found at a single site. The archaeologist methodically counts them, computing the percentage of each type. This yields valuable data on trade between pueblos and on the migration of tribes. The presence of a small amount of Kayenta pottery at a site in New Mexico, mixed with a great deal of Mesa Verde ware, indicates trade between New Mexico and Arizona, for example. A site that has largely Chaco potsherds in the lower levels and Mesa Verde above was probably inhabited by colonists from the Chaco region for a while, then abandoned and later occupied by migrants from Mesa Verde. In this way can history be read from bits of broken pottery.

While the painted pottery of the Pueblos was undergoing these evolutionary changes, even the humble cooking ware was becoming more attractive. The Developmental Pueblo potters, as we have seen, frequently left ridged bands on the necks of their cooking pots for ornamental reasons. Later in the period a corrugated ware became popular, with alternate ridges and depressions formed by pinching the clay with the fingernails. This

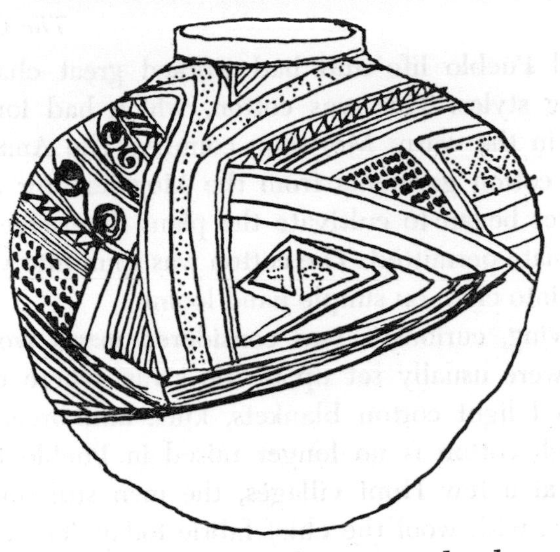

Kayenta black-on-white pottery bowl

style allowed for surprising elegance, and some of the more skillful potters produced strikingly handsome corrugated pots with complicated patterns of ridges.

The great development of Pueblo pottery had generally made basketry a forgotten art by 900 A.D. or so, if one may judge from the scarcity of baskets found in Anasazi sites of the later Developmental period and after. But basketwork is perishable, and many of the Developmental Pueblo sites are open to the elements, while the Basketmaker ruins are found chiefly in sheltered places, so it may simply be that few Developmental baskets have survived. Those that have been found are much more elaborately woven than the Basketmaker types.

Sandals were still being made. The scallop-toed design was replaced with a round-toed pattern. The sandals still were woven from fine yucca fibers, but a new fabric had entered Pueblo life and had worked great changes in clothing styles. This was cotton, which had long been grown in the warm Mogollon country. The Anasazi imported cotton garments from the Mogollon for a while, and later began to cultivate the plant themselves where the climate permitted. The cotton was spun into yarn and woven into cloth on simple hand looms.

Weaving, curiously, was considered man's work. The looms were usually set up in the kivas, where the men produced light cotton blankets, kilts, and breechcloths. Although cotton is no longer raised in Pueblo territory except at a few Hopi villages, the men still do all the weaving, with wool the chief fabric today. The adoption of cotton clothing in the Anasazi towns reduced the need for fur blankets, though some were still made, as well as handsome blankets of feathers, for use in burials. Hair styles began to change, too. The women now allowed their hair to grow long, gathering it into bobs on the sides of their heads.

The basic food was still corn. The ears could be stored like stacked logs after the harvest, and the dried kernels were ground into meal as needed during the months that followed. Beans and squash were still the important secondary crops. The invention of the stone hoe made cultivating the fields easier and produced a bigger yield of food. Pueblo hunters, armed with bows and arrows, brought back bear, elk, buffalo, wolf, mountain sheep, and other animals for meat.

There were changes in pueblo architecture, too. The basic unit was the rectangular room built of stone slabs mortared with mud and roofed with poles and brush.

These units were added together to form great compounds, some with hundreds of rooms. This was the most spectacular achievement of Anasazi civilization. At Chaco Canyon, at Mesa Verde, and at hundreds of other locations throughout the Four Corners area, towering pueblos were constructed, enlarged, modified, repaired—and ultimately abandoned.

The era of the apartment-house dwellers was termed Pueblo III by the Pecos conference of 1927. Some archaeologists still use that designation, but most follow Dr. Frank Roberts' suggestion and call it the Great Pueblo or Classic Pueblo era. Again we must remember that the shift from Developmental Pueblo to Great Pueblo did not happen abruptly, nor did it occur at the same time throughout Anasazi territory. Our labels give the impression of hard and fast divisions, but actually each big phase is the sum of a great many tiny and gradual changes in the life of a village.

The Developmental Pueblo period began, in some places, at about 700 A.D., when the Anasazi came up out of their pit-houses and built their first awkward aboveground dwellings. For the next three centuries certain Anasazi settlements led the way in developing new styles of pottery, in mastering the art of weaving cotton, and in learning how to build pueblos that were more than one story high. By 1000 or 1050 A.D. these pioneering Anasazi groups had changed their way of life in so many ways that we can no longer regard them as Developmental Pueblos. They had entered the Great Pueblo phase.

As always, there were laggards who went about things

in the old fashion for another century or two. At one of the most famous Great Pueblo sites, Chaco Canyon, both traditions seem to have existed side by side. On one side of the canyon rose magnificent Pueblo Bonito, the largest of the Anasazi apartment-houses. Opposite it, a few hundred yards away, was a small, poorly-constructed pueblo in the old style. Perhaps it was occupied by a tribe of stubborn conservatives who would not or could not follow the new trends. They remained a Developmental Pueblo outpost in a Great Pueblo environment.

When we discuss the architectural masterpieces of the Great Pueblo period, we shall be able to offer very exact dates for their construction and for their abandonment. Since the Anasazi kept no written history, it may seem a bit magical to be able to say confidently that a certain pueblo was constructed between 1110 and 1124 A.D., abandoned about 1130, and reoccupied between 1225 and 1252. No magic is involved, though—just an ingenious and extraordinary archaeological technique, which has been mentioned briefly two or three times already and which merits a full explanation here.

The method is called *dendrochronology,* which means "tree-ring dating." It enables archaeologists to assign specific dates to Southwestern ruins by studying the wooden beams with which they were constructed. Dendrochronology is probably the most precise system of archaeological dating yet devised.

It was developed by an astronomer, not an archaeologist. He was Dr. Andrew E. Douglass, who died in 1962 at the age of 94. In 1901 Dr. Douglass was a young astronomer attached to the Lowell Observatory in Arizona, deeply interested in the problem of sunspots. Sunspots are dark blotches of great size that appear on the face of the sun. It had long been known that the number of spots on the sun increases and decreases in a fairly regular cycle, averaging about eleven years from peak to peak. Dr. Douglass was interested in determining whether there was any relation between the sunspot cycles and weather on earth.

Reliable weather records went back only a short time, relatively speaking. Dr. Douglass wanted a way of discovering what the weather had been like five hundred and a thousand years ago, when no one had kept weather charts. As he rode through a forest of tall ponderosa pines near Flagstaff, Arizona, he thought of the growth rings on trees. He knew that each year a tree adds a new layer of wood over its entire living surface. Seen in cross-section, the annual growth pattern appears as a series of ever-expanding rings. In a wet year the ring is broad; in a year of drought it is narrow, since a tree grows less if it lacks nourishment.

Not every kind of tree, Dr. Douglass knew, would provide a clear record of growth rings. Some, such as the ironwood, do not have a regular ring structure. And certain trees would not be useful, because they grow in areas where there is no great variation of moisture from year to year, because of even climate or heavy concentrations of soil water. The long-lived redwood trees of coastal California are useless for this reason, since they lay down rings of approximately the same width every year.

But the pines and firs and hemlocks of the Southwest

were ideal for Dr. Douglass' experiment. There is little soil water in the arid Southwest, so the growth patterns of trees depend almost entirely on the annual rainfall. A year with little rain shows up in the tree-ring record as a narrow ring; a year of frequent downpours leaves a wide ring.

Beginning in 1904, Dr. Douglass began to analyze cross-sections of ponderosa pine from the area around Flagstaff. The trees averaged 348 years old, according to a count of their rings. He measured the width of each ring and found that the sequences of wide and narrow rings corresponded with the local rainfall records. Moreover, the same patterns could be found in every tree. He identified sequences that became familiar to him as he examined more trees: perhaps three wide rings followed by two narrow ones, a wide, two more narrows, two wides, three narrows—a year-by-year record of drought and rainfall. It matched the Flagstaff weather records as far back as those records had been kept. Over the years that followed, Dr. Douglass obtained samples of trees from many parts of the world—fir from Oregon, pine and spruce from Germany, Sweden, Norway, and Great Britain, hemlock from Vermont. His theory about sunspots was confirmed: years with greater-than-usual sunspot activity had produced wide growth rings, indicating heavy rainfall, while the years of low sunspot activity had evidently been years of drought.

By 1915 Douglass had pushed back his analysis of tree-ring patterns far beyond the earliest records of rainfall or sunspots. The pattern still held true. By collecting specimens from the giant sequoia trees of inland California he

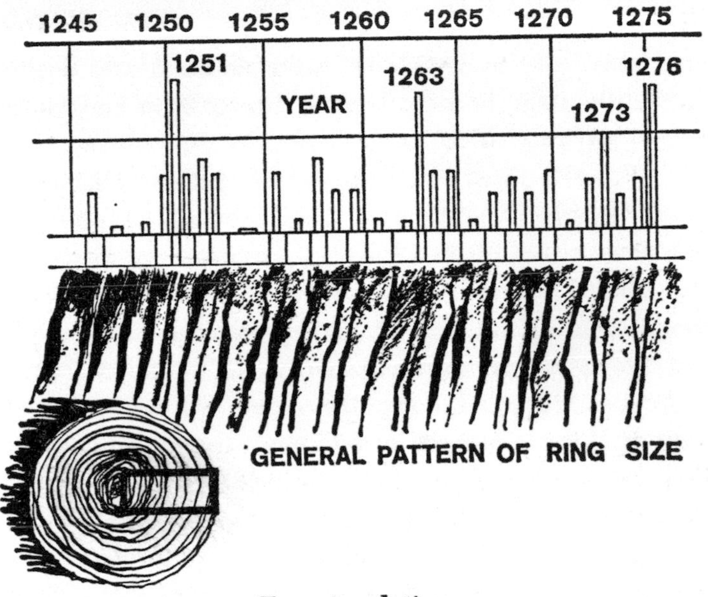

Tree ring dating

was able to extend his observations back 3,000 years, following the 11-year cycle of sunspot activity into the dim past.

Though his basic interest was astronomical, Douglass found he was becoming deeply involved in Southwestern archaeology. Since the oldest living pines in the Southwest were only about 640 years old, he turned to the Pueblo ruins, hoping to add to his record of Southwestern tree-ring patterns by examining ancient logs and timbers that had been used as building materials. From his sections of living trees, he had plotted a tree-ring graph that showed him the relative pattern of rings for the years from 1300 A.D. to 1916. He could compare a section from any living pine of Arizona or New Mexico with his master chart and discover when that tree had begun growing. He could also point to certain rings on his chart and declare confidently that there had been droughts in the Southwest in 1379 or 1672, for example.

In 1916 the American Museum of Natural History allowed Douglass to examine some sections of pine logs from Pueblo Bonito in Chaco Canyon and from the ancient ruined pueblo near Aztec, New Mexico. Three years later he visited the ruin at Aztec and took fifty samples from house-beams, using a special drill that cut out a thin cylinder-shaped core. He glued these samples to wood backings, planed and shaved them smooth, and oiled them to bring out the tree-rings.

He was able to develop a new chart covering some two hundred years. None of the ring-patterns on this chart corresponded to those on his chart of 600-year-old living trees. That told him that the logs at Pueblo Bonito and Aztec had been cut some time before 1300. But how much earlier? He could not say, although he knew that the Aztec beams had been cut about fifty years after those from Pueblo Bonito.

Douglass called this prehistoric chart his "floating chronology." It told a year-by-year story of Southwestern tree growth, but it could not be linked to his living-tree chronology. He realized that if he could join the two chronologies, he would not only have gained much information about ancient weather and sunspot patterns but would provide a startlingly accurate tool for the dating of ancient pueblo ruins.

With the full cooperation of archaeologists, Douglass set out to extend both his floating chronology and his modern chronology, hoping that they would meet and overlap. He received more specimens from Pueblo Bonito, and thereby added 150 years to the floating chronology. From the ruins at Mesa Verde came other samples that provided an entirely new set of ring patterns, matching neither the Pueblo Bonito chart nor the modern chronology. Douglass suspected that the Mesa Verde rings went somewhere between, in the mysterious gap, but at the moment they simply gave him a second floating chronology.

In 1923 Douglass accompanied a National Geographic Society expedition to the Hopi villages of Arizona. These villages had been continuously inhabited since a time before the first Spanish explorations. Douglass hoped that some of the old buildings, particularly those in the ancient Hopi villages of Oraibi and Walpi, might yield timbers that would link his floating chronologies to his modern one.

The Hopi elders were cool to the notion of letting white men drill holes in the beams of their houses. A few specimens were gathered, but they did not close the gap in the chronologies. Though busy with his astronomical duties, Douglass continued a painstaking matching of tree samples from dozens of ruins in Pueblo country. In February, 1928, a cliff house at Betatakin, Arizona, supplied a specimen that matched the latest rings of the Pueblo Bonito chronology and the earliest ones of the Mesa Verde chronology, joining the 350 years of the first to the 180 years of the second. The new floating chronology now covered more than 580 years in continuous prehistoric sequence.

In the same year a second National Geographic expedition visited the Hopi pueblo of Oraibi. Douglass went along, carrying gifts of purple chiffon velvet to win the cooperation of the important men of the community. Renting two rooms in a Hopi house, he wangled permission to take samples from ancient-looking ceiling beams. A log in a kiva, he found, had been cut about 1520. Another, in the pueblo of Walpi, had been cut in 1490. He came to a three-story Oraibi house abandoned in 1906 and now filled with rubbish, and drilled an upright post supporting the ceiling of a second-floor room. It gave a clear series of rings that fit into Douglass' modern chronology and carried it back another forty years, to 1260 A.D. The post had been cut about 1370, Douglass found, which meant that Oraibi had been continuously inhabited for more than 550 years.

Even now, however, the modern chronology could not be linked to the prehistoric floating one. Douglass suspected that the gap was not great. The Oraibi sample indicated that there had been a great drought late in the thirteenth century. The Betatakin and Mesa Verde samples revealed the thin rings of drought at their late ends. Such thin rings could not easily be matched; it was possible that Douglass' two chronologies *did* overlap, but that the faulty rings of the drought period concealed the correspondence.

Some detective work was called for. The Hopi, it seemed, had come to Oraibi at the beginning of the fourteenth century. Where had they lived just previously? If the site could be found, a beam might be discovered that joined the chronologies.

Pottery was the clue. Archaeologists had already determined the sequence of pottery types over the centuries between the Great Pueblo era and the modern Hopi days. The Mesa Verde, Chaco, and Kayenta pottery had been black-on-white, with some red ware at Kayenta. Then the red ware had given way to a polychrome-on-red, and that had evolved into the lovely polychrome-on-cream Hopi pottery of the historic era. The gap in the chronology lay between the Great Pueblo and the historic period. Ruins of pueblos inhabited at a time when the polychrome-on-red was being replaced by the cream-colored ware might hold the answer.

A number of possibilities presented themselves. One site seemed particularly promising, because fragments of an orange-colored transitional pottery had been found there, and because stands of pine grew nearby. It was a ruin at the small town of Showlow, Arizona. Douglass went there in June, 1929. Picking through the rubble, he and the archaeologists who accompanied him cleared away such recent deposits as tin cans and broken pickle bottles to unearth the timber of the prehistoric ruin below. The ancient pueblo had been destroyed by fire centuries ago, and the wood Douglass found was in the form of charcoal—but he had developed techniques for reading the tree-rings even on a bit of charred, blackened wood.

One fragile, badly-burned log seemed to hold the key. Douglass gave it a field label, numbering it Beam HH39, and took it to a nearby house for study. At once he recognized the now-familiar rings of the fourteenth century at the outer end of the beam. He followed inward—1380, 1350, 1300. Now he came to the time of the great drought. He wrote a few months later, "Here were the very small rings that told of the hardships the tree had endured in 1299 and 1295. As we studied the rings further toward the center, 1288, 1286, 1283, and 1280 each told the same story we had found in other beams of lean years and hard living."

The drought rings continued back to 1275. Many rings still remained. They corresponded to the Oraibi beam, but that one ended in 1260, and this one went on and on —1254, 1251, 1247. "Finally," Douglass wrote, "came the one at the very core, and from its central ring we learned that this charred old stick began its life as a promising upright pine, A.D. 1237, just ten years after the Sixth Crusade moved eastward to compel the Saracens to restore Jerusalem."

Late that night, under a sputtering gasoline torch, Douglass labored to link his chronologies. Beam HH39 had carried the historical chronology back twenty-three additional years, from 1260 to 1237. He turned now to the floating chronology. Its 551st ring matched perfectly with that of the ring for the year 1251 in Beam HH39. The gap no longer existed. Douglass now knew that his floating chronology began in 700 A.D., and that its final worn and defective rings actually overlapped with the earliest rings of his Oraibi beam.

Everything fell into place. His oldest Pueblo Bonito timber had been cut in 919, from a tree 219 years old. An important section of Pueblo Bonito had been built in 1067, and the pueblo had still been occupied in 1127. The ruins at Kayenta, Aztec, Mesa Verde and elsewhere could be assigned precise and accurate dates. His discovery was a landmark in archaeology.

Dr. Andrew Douglass continued to study the tree-rings for the rest of his long life. At the time of his death he had lived to see the tree-ring chronology extended back to 11 A.D. His students have successfully developed tree-ring calendars in Alaska, Turkey, and other parts of the world. The most satisfactory use of the system has always been in the Southwest, where a unique combination of circumstances made the development of dendrochronology possible.

Every major ruin of the Pueblo past has now been dated in this way. As we turn to explore some of the monuments of Anasazi architecture, we need not feel that there is anything supernatural in our knowledge of their exact ages.

6

THE APARTMENT-HOUSE BUILDERS

THE GREATEST SINGLE CONCENTRATION of Classic Pueblo ruins is hard to reach, even today. The determined traveler must steel himself for a long, jolting, dusty ride over washboard-rough gravel roads. If he approaches from the north, he will drive through utter solitude for fifty-odd miles after leaving the last town behind. The approach from the south is even more lonely. There are no gas stations along the way, no hamburger stands, no billboards. The wise traveler carries a canteen of fresh water in his car, and fills his gas tank before he sets out. A blown tire can be a catastrophe. Even a sudden downpour can leave him stranded on a road that has turned into an impassable quagmire.

At the end of the journey lies Chaco Canyon National Monument, New Mexico—a long, narrow strip of government-owned land that follows the winding path of the dry, sandy-bedded Chaco Wash. If he arrives here in the summer, as most visitors do, the traveler's impression will be one of heat and dryness. This is a desert. Between the irregular red sandstone walls of the canyon lies a broad, parched plain, more than a mile wide, sandy and forlorn. Tough, scraggly desert plants live here: sagebrush, saltbush, greasewood, rabbitbrush. No trees are in sight. Tiny ground-squirrels scurry across the sand. Slender lizards bask in the hot sunlight and speed away when people approach.

It is a somber, lifeless canyon, where not even tourists care to go. Yet nine centuries ago this valley swarmed with busy men and women. In what is now a barren waste of sand and rock, bitterly cold in winter and fiercely hot in summer, more than a dozen great pueblos were built. A visitor in the year 1100 would have seen a lively vista: men at work in green fields of corn, women squatting before their houses and artfully shaping vessels of clay, naked children chasing one another through the broad plazas, pet dogs barking and pet turkeys gobbling, old men adorned with sumptuous turquoise ornaments solemnly descending into the kivas to speak with the gods. Chaco Canyon throbbed with life.

Then everything changed. The clouds no longer dropped life-giving rain. The stream that was the source of life for the Chaco folk went dry. The fields of corn shriveled. The villagers moved away. The towering pueblos were deserted. Under the merciless eye of the sun the stone buildings crumbled and collapsed and were covered with drifting heaps of hot sand. Chaco Canyon became a land of the dead, fit only for lizards and sagebrush, bone-dry as the Sahara.

The toppled pueblos remained as evidence of the vanished greatness. Hundreds of years went by. Strangers wandered into the canyon, nomads from the north. They were the Navaho, who set up housekeeping at Chaco in the sixteenth century. They looked with superstitious awe at the remains of the old cities, and kept away from them. Those were Anasazi cities, they knew—cities of the Old Ones.

About 1680 a few of the descendants of the Old Ones came back to Chaco. They were refugees from the pueblos along the Rio Grande, who had rebelled against their Spanish overlords. They fled westward to Chaco and built houses on jutting crags upcanyon, but they did not stay long. In a generation or two they were gone, leaving the canyon to its lizards and its squirrels and to the handful of Navaho who occasionally drifted through.

The weather at Chaco changed in the nineteenth century. The rains returned; high grass grew in the canyon. The Navaho began to graze their livestock there. In 1849 a white man arrived: Lieutenant James H. Simpson, who was taking part in a military survey of the Southwest. With nine companions he visited Chaco on August 28, 1849, a few weeks before he stopped to copy the old inscriptions on El Morro. Simpson saw eight ruined pueblos that day, and learned from his Mexican guide the names that had been given them. There was Pueblo Bonito, "Beautiful Town," and Pueblo del Arroyo, "The Town of the Gully," and Casa Chiquita, "The Little House." Some of the ruins had strange Navaho names: Hungo Pavie, Kin Kletso, Chettro Ketl, Kin Nahasbas.

Other explorers, as well as men of the cattle industry, followed Simpson. The livestock of the Carlisle Company grazed in the canyon, while travelers from the east stared in wonder at the dead towns. In 1896 came Richard

Wetherill, the cowboy-turned-archaeologist who was such an important figure in revealing the lost civilization of the Anasazi. He excavated at Pueblo Bonito, partly for scientific information, partly for his own private profit. Wetherill found a wealth of ancient artifacts at Chaco, and sold the collection to two rich easterners, the Hyde brothers, who donated it to the American Museum of Natural History. The Hydes financed a four-year campaign of archaeology from 1897 to 1901, with Wetherill in charge.

Twenty years later came more orthodox archaeologists sponsored by the National Geographic Society. Led by Neil M. Judd, this expedition worked at Pueblo Bonito and neighboring Chaco ruins for many seasons. They carefully uncovered the old buildings, cleared away the rubble, collected the pots and jewelry and utensils of the Old Ones. Judd hired native workmen to help him: Zuni Indians with Anasazi blood in their veins, and Navaho who were probably descended from ancient nomad enemies of the Anasazi. Judd wrote that he had no difficulties "from the simultaneous employment of representatives of these two tribes, hereditary enemies for over 400 years. So far as I could observe, the Zuni were always welcome guests at Navaho homes throughout the valley, and several Navaho were invariably present on Sunday nights when the Zuni danced and sang in the light of a weekly bonfire before our tents."

Today five of the dozen most important Chaco ruins have been excavated completely or in part. The rest remain as time has left them: shapeless mounds overgrown with weeds, out of which jut leaning stone walls. They are reserved for archaeologists of the future, who may have better techniques than those of our day. The excavated ruins have not been rebuilt, merely uncovered and cleared. But the archaeologists have *stabilized* them, which means that they have taken steps to prevent any further deterioration. Tottering walls have been subtly braced; modern cement has replaced much ancient mud mortar. The stabilizing work is still going on, and visitors to the canyon today can watch crews of expert Navaho workmen shoring up the forsaken pueblos of the long-vanished Old Ones.

The ruins of Chaco Canyon number many hundreds, some in the valley, others atop the mesa. The dozen largest ones lie in a single stretch eight miles long and two miles wide, and it is possible to see them all in one day. The grandest of them is Pueblo Bonito. But each of the others has its special fascination.

Pueblo Bonito, even in its present ruined state, is a breathtaking sight. It is so big that the best way to comprehend its shape is to scramble up an ancient Indian trail to the top of the cliff behind it. From there one can see that it is D-shaped, with the curving belly of the D close to the cliff wall, and the backbar looking south across the canyon.

That straight south-facing wall is 518 feet long. A one-story row of rooms ran the length of it; behind it lay a great open plaza in which several kivas were sunk, and beyond was the main section of the pueblo, terrace after terrace of rooms rising in ancient times to a height of five stories. The entire pueblo covered three acres, and contained some 800 rooms. It housed as many as 1,200 people.

Pueblo Bonito was the largest apartment-house in the world for centuries; it was not surpassed until 1882, with the building of the Spanish Flats in New York City. (And the Spanish Flats are gone, demolished to make way for still bigger buildings. Pueblo Bonito remains.)

There are some pit-houses on the south side of the canyon, so we know that Chaco was inhabited in Modified Basketmaker days. Probably the Anasazi began to enter the area about 500 A.D., migrating from the San Juan River region in southern Utah and Colorado. During the time of transition that we call the Developmental Pueblo period, the inhabitants of Chaco Canyon began to build small above-ground pueblos. These gradually grew more imposing during the eighth and ninth centuries.

Some time about 900 A.D. construction began on a new pueblo along the north wall of the canyon. It was built right over the site of a pit-house village. This first section of Pueblo Bonito was small and untidy, as though its builders were still unsure of their craft. They used sandstone slabs that they chopped down to a standard width by hammering away the sides. This left the edges of the slabs thinner than the middles, and to make the slabs stack evenly the builders employed thick gobs of adobe mud mortar, and wedged little chips of rock between the big stone slabs to protect the mortar from the rain and from the eroding effects of wind-blown sand.

It was sloppy masonry, but everything was plastered over with an outer coating of mud, so no one had to look at the irregular, lopsided stonework. As the population grew, more rooms were added to the right and left of the old ones. The cluster of houses gradually took on a crescent shape, curving away from the canyon wall. Tree-ring dates tell us that the oldest surviving roof-timbers of this section of Pueblo Bonito were cut in 919 A.D.

Many years later—as late as 1050, perhaps—newcomers arrived in Chaco Canyon. They also came from the area north of the San Juan. We have no idea what spurred them to look for new homes. They were Anasazi too, but they were more advanced, more skillful than the Pueblo Bonito people. The archaeologist Neil M. Judd calls them the Late Bonitians, to distinguish them from the Old Bonitians who already occupied Chaco Canyon.

The Late Bonitians did not build a new pueblo of their own. They simply moved into Pueblo Bonito and took it over. The Old Bonitians, outnumbered by this swarm of aggressive, alert strangers, were helpless. Soon they found the Late Bonitians adding dozens of rooms to the pueblo, extending it greatly from the original core of Old Bonitian rooms.

The masonry of the Late Bonitians was enormously superior to that of the older inhabitants. Instead of simply piling odd-shaped slabs of stone to make a wall, the Late Bonitians built a core of rubble and adobe and faced it on both sides with blocks of sandstone that had been squared off on their outer surfaces. At first the Late Bonitians used blocks of unequal size and shape, and plugged the chinks with little pieces of sandstone about a quarter of an inch thick. Later they used uniform sandstone slabs a few inches thick, which they alternated with inch-thick tablets to make a pleasing decorative effect. Finally the master masons of Pueblo Bonito grew so

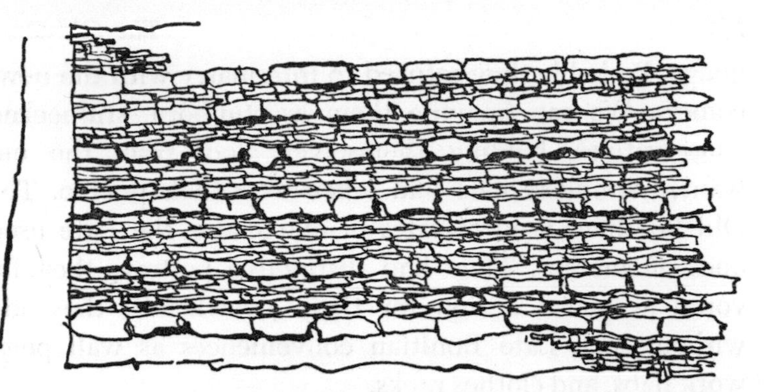

Pueblo Bonito masonry, Chaco Canyon

capable that they dispensed with all the thin stone inserts and faced their walls with sandstone blocks of equal size, fitted so closely together that hardly any adobe mortar was needed. Hardly anyone in the Southwest built better walls than these Late Bonitians. Yet they covered their first-rate work with a plaster of mud, concealing it just as though it were the crude, sloppy work of the Old Bonitians. Only today, when none of the plaster coating remains, can we see the four styles of Bonitian masonry side by side and appreciate the increasing skill of these vanished craftsmen.

Late Bonitians and Old Bonitians lived close together in the growing city. But there does not seem to have been much mingling of the two populations. Huddling in their ramshackle rooms at the back of the pueblo, the Old Bonitians went on making pottery and utensils in their own style, generations after the Late Bonitians had come to live with them. Very likely they worshipped in their own kivas and had different ceremonies from the Late Bonitians. They may have spoken a different language. Probably they refused to intermarry with the newcomers. We can imagine them as stubborn, stiffnecked conservatives, holding themselves aloof from the unwanted strangers who had taken over their pueblo. The Old Bonitians used metates of one shape, the Late used ones of another. They had distinctive pottery; they favored a special design for their arrowheads; they did without such Late Bonitian conveniences as wall pegs, work slabs, and clothes racks.

Living conditions were cramped in both parts of the pueblo. The rooms were small and dark. The ceilings were about seven feet high in the Old Bonitian section, a foot higher in the Late Bonitian. Though some of the Late Bonitian rooms were as big as ten feet by sixteen in floor area, most of the families in the pueblo were crowded into rooms eight by ten and even smaller. Each family had a room for storage and one that served for eating, sleeping, and living. When possible the people stayed outdoors. Since there were no chimneys, they could not have fireplaces in their rooms, and all cooking was done in the plaza.

There were no stairways; the people in the upper stories had to scramble up ladders to reach their rooms. The pueblo did not have corridors, either, so those who lived in the back rooms had to march through the homes of five or six families to get to their own. Privacy was at a minimum in Pueblo Bonito.

The life of the pueblo depended on farming. Since rainfall was sparse and unpredictable in Chaco Canyon at the best of times, the people used the "floodwater" method of irrigation. They placed their fields in the paths of rainwater running from higher locations, or built low earth dams to store the water of the flash floods that sometimes came down Chaco Wash. The usual Pueblo crops were grown: corn, beans, squash. Bonitian huntsmen preyed on the mule deer, bobcat, mountain sheep, grizzly bear, and other local animals.

The turkey and the dog had long since been tamed by the Anasazi. When Coronado reached the Zuni pueblos in 1540, he reported that Zuni turkeys tasted "very good, and better than those of Mexico," but the Pueblo people themselves did not eat the birds. They used the whites of the eggs in their paint, and the turkey feathers to make handsome robes and blankets. The bones of dead turkeys were whittled into needles and awls. Turkey flesh itself, and that of fowl of all kinds, have been taboo among the Pueblos until very recently.

The women of Pueblo Bonito produced excellent pottery, as the vast trash-heap of the ruin testifies. Several huge mounds in front of the south wall of Pueblo Bonito contain twenty-foot-deep layers of refuse accumulated over centuries. Like all archaeologists, Neil Judd turned eagerly to this hoard of rubbish at the outset of his work at Pueblo Bonito in 1921. By digging a trench downward through the dump, he could identify the different styles of Bonitian pottery—the earliest, of course, being at the bottom of the heap.

When Judd drove his trench into the dump he got strange and disturbing results. Near the surface he found potsherds of a type that elsewhere had been identified as late Classic Pueblo style. Below them were sherds of a recognizably earlier sort. He kept digging—and found late-type sherds *below* early-type ones! Something was very wrong. This trash-heap drama threatened to upset all that was known about Anasazi pottery styles. Not until 1925 did Judd have the answer. Further excavation revealed that a huge kiva had once been northwest of the rubbish heap. It had been built by the Late Bonitians, who had excavated an area about 50 feet in diameter. The site selected for the kiva adjoined an Old Bonitian rubbish heap. The kiva-builders had simply scooped up the rubbish that was in their way, dumping it on top of a newer rubbish heap nearby, and so early potsherds were found to be resting above later ones. In time that big kiva had been filled in and other buildings had risen above it, for the Late Bonitians restlessly built and rebuilt their pueblo constantly.

The pueblo grew year after year. Sometimes the city planners changed their minds; Judd uncovered foundations which indicated that an entire wing of the pueblo had been added and then torn down, its stones being used elsewhere. One place that drew special attention was right behind the pueblo's eastern corner. A titanic slab of rock, weighing more than 100,000 tons, had been detached from the cliff by the action of rain and wind, and stood alone, seemingly ready to topple at any moment and crush the pueblo. The Bonitians built a framework of low walls at the base of this vast rock. They did not think they could actually hold the rock back with their puny brace of stone and mud and sticks; apparently they were merely trying to halt erosion at the base of the rock so as to keep it from falling forward onto the pueblo.

The rock did not fall. It still stood when the Navaho

came into Chaco Canyon centuries after the Anasazi had departed, and gave the ruin the name of *Tse-biya hani ahi,* "Place of the Braced-up Cliff." The white men called the menacing slab Threatening Rock. After Chaco Canyon became a national monument early in the twentieth century, park rangers eyed Threatening Rock worriedly and studied ways of permanently bracing it. It did not seem possible. Finally, on January 22, 1941, during a harsh winter, the precariously balanced tower of rock gave way. It crashed forward onto the fragile ruins of Pueblo Bonito, and through the valley there echoed a sound like the explosion of a mighty bomb.

"Until the dust cleared," said a ranger who was there at the time, "we didn't know if Bonito was still there or not." Luckily most of the ruin was unharmed. But 100 feet of the spectacular back wall was destroyed, and 30 excavated rooms were buried. The fragments of the colossal rock, themselves giant boulders, still cover the corner of the ruin today.

The most recent tree-ring date at Pueblo Bonito is 1130 A.D. No construction was done there after that year. Conditions changed in Chaco Canyon, and the Bonitians began to leave.

The Late Bonitians were the first to go, apparently. Dr. Judd found several feet of sand on the floors of many Late Bonitian rooms in the pueblo, with the masonry of the collapsed upper stories on top. This told him that those rooms had been abandoned and allowed to fill with wind-blown sand long before the building became a ruin. The Old Bonitians continued to occupy their ancient homes. They used the abandoned rooms of the Late Bonitians as storage chambers and as trash-dumps; Old Bonitian refuse was found above layers of blown sand in some Late Bonitian rooms. Family after family of Late Bonitians struck out for greener pastures in an evacuation that may have lasted twenty or thirty years, and still the Old Bonitians remained.

Why did the Late Bonitians leave?

One possibility is that Chaco Canyon was under attack by tribes of warlike nomads. The giant pueblo had been built in an open plain, and enemies could easily swoop through it. Originally the Old Bonitians had built no doors in the outer walls of their pueblo. When the Late Bonitians came the valley must have been at peace, for they confidently built doors in the back wall, not only on the upper stories but on ground level as well. Soon those doors were plugged with slabs of stone, as though the Late Bonitians realized the danger of leaving entrances for attackers. They never again built any doorway in an outer wall of the pueblo. In time even the town gate in front was sealed, so that no one could enter except by climbing a ladder to the second story.

We can envision howling bands of savages surrounding the sealed-up pueblo, battering at its walls, trying to scramble over the barriers. War parties must have broken through from time to time, racing furiously through the courtyards of Pueblo Bonito, striking down the peaceful farmers who tried to defend their homes. It was too much for the Late Bonitians; they began to abandon the pueblo. The Old Bonitian families stayed behind, fearful and uncertain. Now it became hazardous even to venture out to till the fields. Once the dead had been buried in some

I. Spruce Tree House, showing kiva roof construction. Mesa Verde National Park, Colorado.

II–III. Spruce Tree House.

IV. Cliff Palace, Mesa Verde National Park.

V. An excavated pit-house, Mesa Verde National Park.

VI. Sun Temple, Mesa Verde National Park. The tops of the Pueblo-built walls have since been covered with a layer of cement to preserve the structure.

VII. Petroglyph found at Petrified Forest National Park, Arizona.

NEW MEXICO STATE TOURIST BUREAU

VIII. An Indian of Jemez pueblo, New Mexico.

IX–X Pueblo petroglyphs on Newspaper Rock, Petrified Forest National Park.

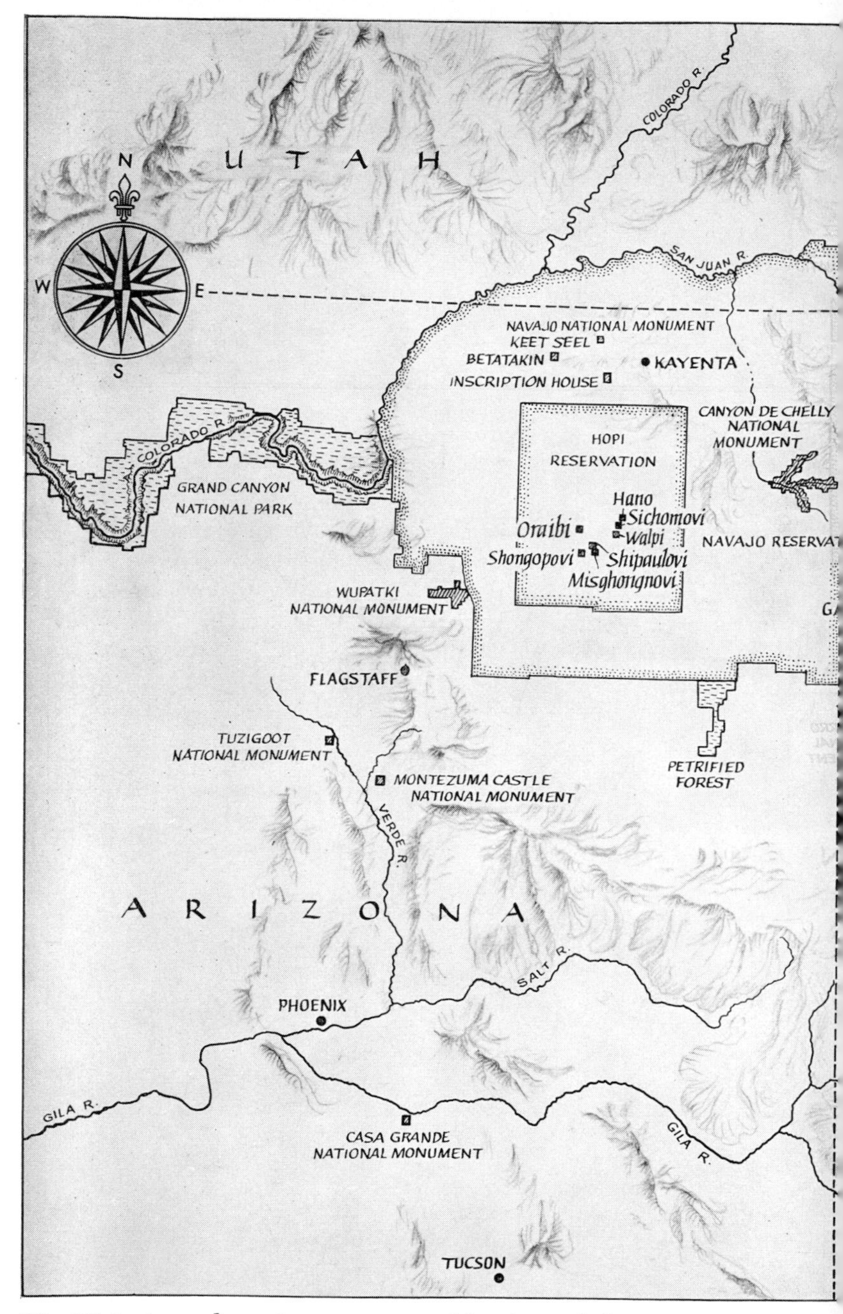

XI. Historic and contemporary pueblo sites of the American Southwest.

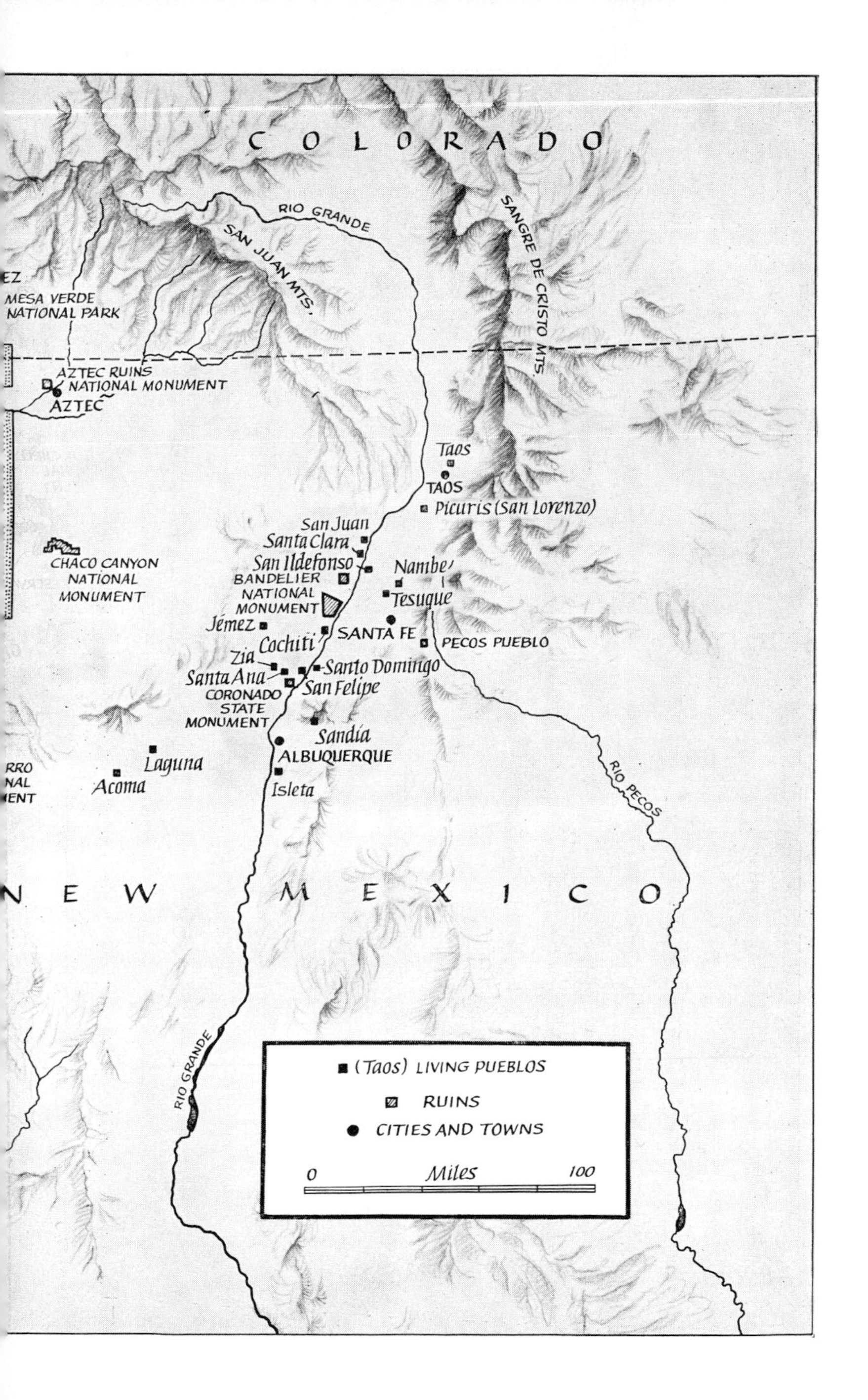

COLORADO
RIO GRANDE
SAN JUAN MTS.
SANGRE DE CRISTO MTS.
MESA VERDE
NATIONAL PARK
AZTEC RUINS
NATIONAL MONUMENT
AZTEC
Taos
TAOS
Picuris (San Lorenzo)
San Juan
Santa Clara
San Ildefonso
Nambe
BANDELIER
NATIONAL
MONUMENT
Tesuque
CHACO CANYON
NATIONAL
MONUMENT
Jémez
SANTA FE
Cochiti
PECOS PUEBLO
Zia
Santo Domingo
Santa Ana
San Felipe
CORONADO
STATE
MONUMENT
Sandía
ALBUQUERQUE
Laguna
Acoma
Isleta
RIO PECOS
NEW MEXICO
RIO GRANDE
(Taos) LIVING PUEBLOS
RUINS
CITIES AND TOWNS
0
Miles
100

XII. Chettro Ketl, Chaco Canyon National Monument, New Mexico.

XIII. Great Kiva at Chettro Ketl.

XIV. Pueblo Bonito, Chaco Canyon National Monument.

XV. Tyuonyi Ruin, Bandelier National Monument, New Mexico.

XVI. Excavated ruins at Picuris Pueblo, New Mexico.

XVII. The author entering an underground kiva at Picuris Pueblo.

XVIII–XIX. Taos Pueblo, New Mexico.

XX. *Taos Pueblo, showing protruding roof beams.*

XXI. *Navajo winter hogan (left) and summer dwelling, Canyon de Chelly National Monument, Arizona.*

NEW MEXICO DEPARTMENT OF DEVELOPMENT

XXII. An Indian woman of Isleta, New Mexico, grinding corn between the flat metate *stone and the* mano *in her hands.*

NEW MEXICO DEPARTMENT OF DEVELOPMENT

XXIII. Dominga Chewiwi, an Indian matriarch of Isleta.

graveyard far from the pueblo, but that was too risky now, and the Old Bonitians laid their dead to rest beneath the floors of their homes. One room alone was the burial place for 24 bodies in shallow, hastily-dug graves.

Probably there was a second reason for abandoning the pueblo, even more pressing than nomad invasion. The canyon was growing dry and barren. From 1090 to 1101, the tree-rings tell us, there was one drought after another at Chaco. The fields of corn withered. There were no floods to moisten the ground.

And the Anasazi themselves had changed the environment of Chaco Canyon for the worse. When they had arrived, thick stands of pine and fir grew in the canyon, but they had felled thousands of trees for the roof beams of Pueblo Bonito and Chettro Ketl and the other huge towns. The timber found in the pueblos showed no scars indicating that it had been cut a great distance away and hauled to Chaco Canyon. It was local wood.

When all the trees of the canyon were gone, no root systems remained to slow the rush of flood waters in the wet years. Now the spring floods came sluicing through the canyons, scouring away the fertile topsoil and exposing the bare rock below. The floods moved so fast through the now-treeless valley that a deep arroyo, or gully, was cut. It became the only channel for the water that once had swirled over the entire canyon floor. The shrubs and grass beyond the edges of the arroyo died of thirst, and, with that ground cover gone, the flood runoff became even faster. In dry years, no moisture; in wet years, savage floods ripping down the arroyo. The fields of Chaco Canyon became useless. Harried by nomads, bewildered by the rapid transformation of their fertile valley into a desert, the Bonitians moved on to other parts of the Four Corners region. Perhaps a dozen families still remained in the great pueblo by 1150, paralyzed by fear, victims of the marauders who entered Bonito again and again and escaped with corn, slaves, even the jewels that adorned the bodies of the dead.

The other pueblos of Chaco were being abandoned too. At the height of the canyon's glory, late in the eleventh century, all these towns were simultaneously inhabited, giving the valley a total population of thousands. Some of the nearby pueblos were nearly as impressive as Pueblo Bonito itself. Not far to the east was Chettro Ketl, which had been built between 1030 and 1116 A.D. This D-shaped pueblo had over five hundred rooms, and its masonry was superior even to that at Bonito. Along the front wall of Chettro Ketl the builders had arranged groups of sandstone slabs in vertical rows to make striking colonnades. At Chettro, also, were several "great kivas"—subterranean circular rooms much bigger than ordinary kivas. The great kivas at Chettro Ketl, now excavated, are some 60 feet in diameter. A great kiva at Pueblo Bonito was only slightly smaller. The biggest of all is across the canyon. Called Casa Rinconada, it is 63 feet in diameter.

Another important Chaco town was Pueblo del Arroyo, a quarter of a mile west of Pueblo Bonito—a suburb, so to speak. It had 284 rooms and 17 kivas, arranged in a D-shaped block around an open court. This village was built between 1052 and 1117; by 1130 it may have been deserted.

While the exodus from Chaco was going on, one band

of Anasazi seems to have moved *into* the canyon. They came from the north, from Mesa Verde country, and built a pueblo west of Bonito. It is known today by the Navaho name of Kin Kletso. It is totally unlike the other pueblos of Chaco Canyon. The others are large and sprawling, centering around big open plazas. There is no plaza at Kin Kletso. The building is small, compact, forbidding-looking. Behind its walls lies a maze of little rooms and kivas, crammed tightly together. Kin Kletso has yielded tree-ring dates as late as 1178, almost half a century later than the most recent at Bonito and Chettro Ketl. We can picture these latecomers as doggedly building their town despite the menace of nomad raids, and we can see them hauling up the ladders every night, settling down behind their doorless walls. Kin Kletso must have closed up like a turtle once night fell. But a time came when these people had to leave Chaco too, and when they were gone, the valley fell silent.

THE TRAIL OF THE CHACO PEOPLE after they abandoned their great pueblos is a complicated one. The Hopi have a tradition that says they were the builders of the Chaco towns. According to this legend, the Flute Clan and Snake Clan of the Hopi came to Chaco first. To keep the valley fertile, they held races each year; a priest carrying a jar of sacred water would run through the canyon, and the fastest men of each clan would try to catch him. The sacred water would bring rain to the fields of the clan that caught him.

In time, say the Hopi, more and more clans entered the canyon. The big pueblos were built. The annual races lost their sacred character and became mere sporting events. As a result, rain became scarce and the springs began to dry up. The elders of the clans came together and decided that they must leave the canyon and migrate elsewhere, as a penance for having allowed the ceremonies to be corrupted.

The Hopi clans left the valley separately. The Flute Clan settled in a place called Suyatupovi ("Where the Soil is Soft"), now known as Canyon de Chelly. The Snake, Fire, and Sun Clans went farther to the northwest, and built the cliff houses near Kayenta. Eventually all the Hopi were reunited on the mesas they now occupy in eastern Arizona.

Probably there is some truth in these Hopi tales. But the Hopi do not mention the great pueblo at Aztec, New Mexico, which is almost certainly one of the places that the Chaco people went after abandoning the canyon.

Aztec is some sixty miles northeast of Chaco Canyon. It is poorly named, for there were never any Aztecs here. When white settlers built a town there in the nineteenth century, they found ruins and thought they were the work of the Aztec Indians of Mexico. They called their town Aztec, and the ruins became known as "those ruins at Aztec." They are still called Aztec Ruins today, though we know that they were an Anasazi settlement.

Aztec is near the Animas River, a tributary of the San Juan. Quite likely the area was inhabited in Basketmaker and Developmental Pueblo times, but not much is yet known about the early archaeology of the district. In the first quarter of the twelfth century, a big pueblo began to rise very rapidly in the Animas Valley. Tree-ring dates

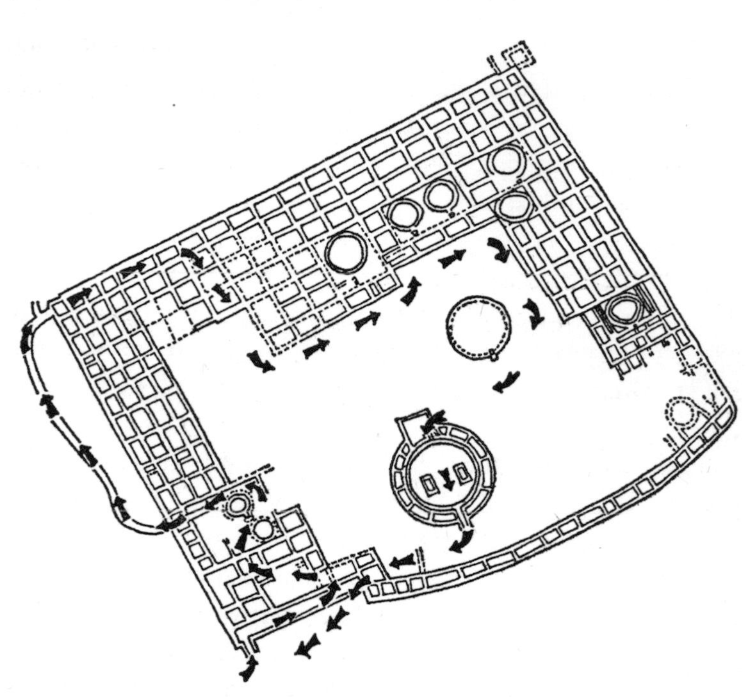

Ground plan of Aztec Ruins

show that it was built between 1110 and 1124, an extremely short period of construction. Unlike Pueblo Bonito, which grew Topsy-fashion over several centuries, Aztec was a well-planned village, three stories high in some places, around a central plaza.

We cannot definitely say that Aztec was built by refugees from Chaco Canyon, but that seems likely. The masonry is of the high quality associated with Pueblo Bonito and Chettro Ketl. The sandstone slabs are neatly dressed, and along the 278-foot west wall there is a narrow band of green sandstone that probably was intended as a decoration. Aztec pottery, too, follows the Chaco styles. It would appear that a sizable band of Anasazi, driven from Chaco Canyon by drought, gullies, and enemy invasion, came to Aztec about 1100 and quickly built an extensive new village for themselves.

Here they lived in the familiar Anasazi fashion. As we stand in the broad plaza today, we can imagine a scene of bustling activity: women kneeling before metates to grind corn, others making pottery, men and boys in the fields, oldsters swapping stories of the Chaco Canyon days.

Then they left. They had been at Aztec hardly a generation. It was about 1130 when they moved on, this time to parts unknown. At about the same time the last stragglers were clearing out of Pueblo Bonito and Chettro Ketl. We think that drought and arroyo-cutting were important factors in driving the Anasazi out of Chaco, but there was no shortage of water at Aztec, because the Animas has always been a substantial stream. Perhaps the nomads who were attacking Pueblo Bonito were also raiding Aztec. Or possibly there was some religious reason, unfathomable to us, that compelled the people of Aztec to abandon their new and solidly-built pueblo.

They moved on, and the wind whipped through the empty pueblo, and the rooms filled with sand. Beams gave way here and there. The walls slowly crumbled. For a full century the village stood abandoned. Then it knew life again. A tribe from the north arrived, migrants from the Mesa Verde area. About 1225 they came to Aztec, and exercised squatters' rights on the deserted ruin.

These Mesa Verde folk rebuilt Aztec after their own fashion. They preferred to live in smaller rooms with lower ceilings, so they partitioned some of the Chaco-style rooms and built new ones of their own. Their masonry was poor compared with that of the earlier builders, and so it is easy today to see which parts of the pueblo were constructed by the Chaco folk and which by the ones who came down from Mesa Verde. Some of the old rooms were dismantled and their building-stones used for new dwellings. The kivas were repaired, but the new arrivals built kivas of their own in a style a little different from that of Chaco; they preferred a keyhole shape to the circular plan of the other people. The trash-heaps of Aztec began to rise high once more, and this time they abounded in the thick-walled potsherds of the Mesa Verde type, above the layers of the thin Chaco style.

There was a great kiva at Aztec, with a diameter of 48 feet. Like those at Chaco Canyon, it differed considerably from the ordinary small kivas. Instead of entering this great kiva by ladder through the roof smoke-hole, the worshippers used a passage at the southern side of the deep chamber. Fourteen small rooms encircled the kiva at surface level. These may have been dressing rooms used to store the masks and costumes worn during the religious ceremonies. Four big columns of masonry and logs, resting atop thick disks of stone, supported the 90-ton roof. There was a large fire-pit in the center of the great kiva; a pair of stone-lined vaults flanked it. The purpose of these sunken vaults is not known today. They may have been used as sweat baths in purification rites, or possibly they were covered with hides or boards, and served as big drums whose booming reverberations echoed ominously through the huge underground building.

When the Mesa Verde people moved into Aztec, they

repaired the great kiva in a sloppy, half-hearted way. Maybe they had no use for it, since at Mesa Verde there are hardly any great kivas. Apparently the Mesa Verde folk preferred to use smaller, single-clan kivas.

After they had occupied Aztec a few years, the Mesa Verde people stopped holding ceremonies in the great kiva. The community now had a new religious center, which has been excavated and can be seen a few hundred feet behind the main ruin. This was a building of a strange and distinctive type which archaeologists call a "Tri-wall structure." It may have been the shrine of a Mexican cult that influenced Anasazi life late in the Classic Pueblo period.

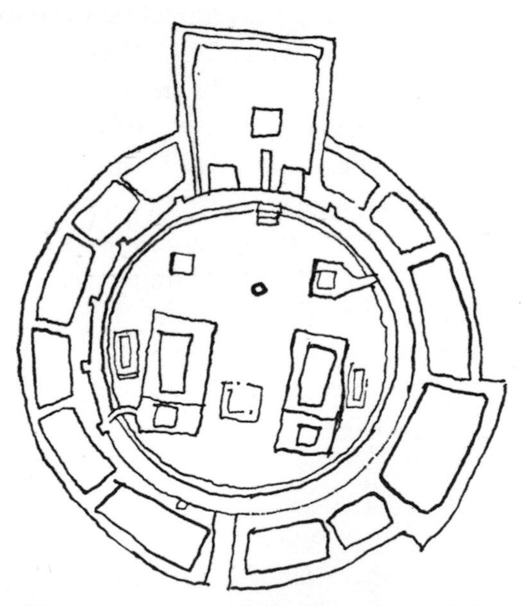

Floor plan of the Great Kiva, Aztec Ruins

Not many of these Tri-wall structures are known. One adjoins Pueblo del Arroyo in Chaco Canyon. Two are at Aztec—the large one that has been cleared, and an unexcavated mound. A fourth, not yet explored by archaeologists, is at Chacra Mesa, south of Chaco Canyon. Another, near Cortez, Colorado, was discovered in 1878 but is now overgrown by weeds, as are three double-walled buildings found at the same time. In 1955 a possible Tri-wall structure was found at Mesa Verde.

To anyone familiar with Anasazi ruins, with their regular rows of rectangular rooms, there is something mysterious and even faintly sinister about the Tri-walls. The big one at Aztec was built over two earlier levels, an adobe village of the Developmental period and a slightly later cluster of rooms and kivas. The Tri-wall is 64 feet in diameter, with massive walls now seven feet high forming three concentric rings. Partitions were built to divide the spaces between the outer two rings into rooms; there are eight rooms in the inner circle, fourteen in the outer one. At the very heart of the structure is a kiva whose wall is separate from the innermost ring of the Tri-wall.

The Tri-wall at Pueblo del Arroyo is 73 feet in diameter, with six rooms in the inner circle, ten in the outer. There was no inner kiva, simply an open plaza 21 feet across. It is older than the one at Aztec; tree-ring dates indicate that it was built about 1109. The Aztec Tri-wall has not yet been dated, but the presence of Mesa Verde pottery types shows that it was built in the middle of the thirteenth century.

Some archaeologists have suggested that these curious buildings were the temples of the Mexican god Quetzalcoatl, who was worshipped through much of Mexico and Central America in various forms. This is only a guess, and so far there is not much real proof behind it. Certainly, though, the Tri-walls represented some new, sharp break with Anasazi traditions.

The Pueblo people have never had a class of full-time priests. Everyone in the community takes part in the religious ceremonies. Some men are older and wiser than the rest, and know the rituals better; they are the leaders. But they do not live in special houses, and when the festivals are over the elders live and work as ordinary members of the pueblo. Except for the chief himself, no man or group of men has purely religious functions, lives apart from the others, and is supported by the labor of the rest of the village.

Dr. R. Gordon Vivian of the National Park Service, the archaeologist who excavated the big Tri-wall at Aztec in 1953, thinks that the unusual structure may have been the residence of a newly-developed priestly class. He suggests that the priests of this new cult lived in the small rooms surrounding the center of the Tri-wall, away from the villagers. But if such a religious revolution did take place, it was short-lived. By the end of the thirteenth century the Anasazi were migrating again, spurred by drought, and no Tri-walls are found in the regions where they built their new pueblos.

Aztec was abandoned for the second time in about 1300. The record of the tree-rings tells of the bad times: year after year of drought from 1276 to 1299. Drought alone would not have been enough to force the Anasazi from Aztec, but there were other hardships. Fire broke out in the east wing of the pueblo and destroyed many rooms. Whole clans were left homeless, and preferred to migrate rather than to rebuild. The troublesome nomads assailed the village. When the people left, it was a quick departure. They sealed all doors and windows as though they planned to return someday and wanted to protect the things they were leaving behind. Once more they took to the road. This time no new occupants moved in. For centuries Aztec stood empty.

In 1859 came the first recorded visit to the ruins since the great migration. Dr. John Strong Newberry, a versatile man who had taken degrees in both medicine and geology, arrived at Aztec as part of an exploring team ranging the entire Southwest. "The principal structures," he wrote, "are large pueblos handsomely built of stone, and in a pretty good state of preservation. The external walls are composed of yellow Cretaceous sandstone, dressed to a common smooth surface without hammer-marks; in some places they are still 25 feet in height." He entered some of the rooms, which were "in a perfect state of preservation, and handsomely plastered."

About twenty-five years later a local schoolteacher led a party of boys into the ruins. They dug up skulls, pottery, turquoise beads, stone axes, and many other relics of the Old Ones. The yield was so good that the people of Aztec came to regard the ruins as their private antiquity-mine. They plundered the rooms at will, removing artifacts of priceless archaeological importance. Finally the vandalism was halted, and in 1916 the first scientific excavation began there under Earl H. Morris. Five years later the ruins were designated a national monument, and now are protected by the government. Despite the raids carried out by the townsfolk, much of the pueblo was untouched when Morris began his work, and a great deal is still awaiting excavation.

In 1933 and 1934 Morris was given the task of restoring the great kiva. Though the National Park Service does not usually attempt to reconstruct the ancient ruins, it occasionally rebuilds some single feature of a site to give an idea of its appearance in Anasazi days. Today, visitors to Aztec can enter the great kiva and see it much as it probably was about the year 1120. Standing in the deep, dark room, they can let their imaginations rove freely, conjuring up pictures of priests in colorful robes, of chanting worshippers, of flickering fires casting their glow on the altar.

What rites were performed in that vast chamber, and in the strange Tri-wall outside the pueblo, will always remain time's secret. So, too, will the reasons for the abrupt departure of the Anasazi from the great apartment-houses. The buildings themselves remain, roofless, shattered, enigmatic. Yellow-brown Aztec, dark-brown Pueblo Bonito, somber Kin Kletso, sprawling Chettro Ketl, all stand dead and empty and awesome in the bright New Mexico sunlight.

7

THE CLIFF-DWELLERS

IN THE YEARS FROM 1050 to 1130, the most dynamic center of Anasazi life was undoubtedly Chaco Canyon. The Great or Classic Pueblo era can be said to have begun in Chaco. The massive apartment-houses constructed there and at Aztec are the grandest works of the Anasazi builders.

But there was an older Anasazi settlement well to the north, perhaps the oldest of all. The Old Ones had lived there from earliest Basketmaker days, gradually growing toward the Pueblo culture. While their distant cousins of Chaco Canyon were flinging up their giant pueblos, these northern people were building smaller apartment-houses in somewhat the same manner. And after Chaco had been abandoned, the northerners began to construct pueblos of a new type. They cannot match those of Chaco for size, but they have such otherworldly grace and splendor that they have become the most famous of Anasazi dwellings. These are the cliff-houses of Mesa Verde: castles in the sky, airy villages nestling in shallow niches high above the canyons.

A Spaniard gave Mesa Verde its name about two hundred years ago. He came to a region of deep canyons and flat mountains covered with thick forests of juniper and pinyon pine. It looked like a "green tableland," a *mesa verde,* to him and to everyone else who has ever seen it. The many mesas of Mesa Verde are like long fingers pointing south toward New Mexico from the high plateau of southern Colorado.

This is the heart of the Four Corners country. From a lookout point on the twisting road that leads to the ruins of Mesa Verde, the traveler can see all four of the states that meet here. It is cool country, not nearly so hot or so dry as Chaco, and the first Basketmakers must have reaped good harvests from the crops that they planted in the fertile soil of the mesa-tops.

The full course of Anasazi development can be seen in a few hours of driving along Chapin Mesa. Here are the pit-houses; here are the first rows of pueblos; here are the growing villages. We can see the entire sequence. At one point is the ruin of a slab-house pueblo built about 850. It consists of a row of rooms whose floors are a foot or more below ground level. The walls are lined with slabs of stone at their foundations, and above the slabs are slender posts, a few inches apart, with adobe filling the spaces between them. In front of the pueblo are four pit-houses, each about six feet deep.

Only a few feet away is a post-and-adobe pueblo built fifty years later. Its floors are at ground level, and there are no stone slabs. The posts in the walls are a foot apart, and the adobe filling is strengthened with a chinking of small stones. Here, too, are some pit-houses, but they are beginning to look like kivas; they have benches encircling their adobe-plastered walls, and posts rising along the walls instead of from the middle of the floors, to support the roofs.

Practically on top of this ruin is a masonry pueblo dating from the year 950. Its walls are of stone and adobe, but there is as much mud as there is stone in the wall, and the sandstone slabs are irregular in shape, laid in crooked rows. There is a kiva here, with mud-plastered walls; it has four stone pillars as roof supports, resting on the bench that circles the chamber.

Further advance is shown in the next ruin, a pueblo built of single-coursed masonry. It dates from 1000 A.D. The stones are well shaped and laid in even rows, but their outer surfaces have been left rough. The walls are the thickness of a single slab less than a foot in width. The kiva, too, has stone walls, and six stone pillars to brace the roof.

The fifth in this series of ruins was built about 1075 A.D. It is a pueblo of double-coursed masonry. We can see the marks of the stone hammers used to shape the sandstone of the walls. The faces of the building-blocks have been cut smooth, and the blocks are stacked two by two to form the walls. Not much mortar has been needed to bind the blocks together, which shows what a good job the ancient masons now were capable of doing. Many of the walls are two stories high. The kiva has eight stone roof-supports, and adjoining the kiva is a large stone tower three stories high. An underground passage connects it with the kiva.

We are not certain what function these tall round

towers served at Mesa Verde. Since they are connected with the kivas in most instances, they may have had some religious use. Or they may have been watchtowers from whose tops lookouts could scan the mesa for the approach of enemies. The development of these kiva-towers is one example of the ceaseless experimentation in pueblo design that went on at Mesa Verde from 750 to 1100 A.D. The sequence of ruins we have just seen shows what a time of change and experiment this was. Building materials and pueblo design improved; mud and posts gave way to stone walls; the kiva evolved out of the pit-house. The mesa-top villages flourished. It must have been a time of peace, for there were hundreds of small towns in the Mesa Verde area, all of them built in open, exposed sites on top of the mesas.

About 1100 a new village pattern began to appear. The old villages with their open sites were abandoned, and were succeeded by pueblos that were more compact, with massive double-coursed walls. The new structures were terraced and several stories tall, with no doorways into the ground-floor rooms except such as faced protected courtyards. The kivas, which once had been built in open areas in front of the villages, now were placed in the heart of the pueblos, surrounded by rooms or walled-in courts. Every village had its tower, rising high above the dwellings.

These new pueblos looked more like fortresses than villages. There can be little doubt that warrior tribes had begun to raid Mesa Verde. The population began to decline. Many acres of farmland on the mesa-tops were given back to the forest. Old pueblos were torn down and their building-blocks used to make the new ones more secure. About 1200 the Mesa Verde people found it necessary to take an even more drastic defensive step. They left the mesa-tops altogether. After seven hundred years of progress, the Anasazi went back to the caves.

These caves were different from the small shallow shelters in which the Basketmakers lived. They were great high vaults in the sides of cliffs, protected by huge stone overhangs, but open to the sun. These caves were not deep—it might be no more than sixty or seventy feet from the rim of a cave to the back wall—but they were so high and broad that an entire pueblo could be built in one.

So the strange and wonderful cliff-houses were built. Some were big enough to house hundreds of people; others had no more than three or four rooms. In every cranny of the Mesa Verde cliffs the new houses rose, always in hard-to-reach places whose trails needed only a few warriors to guard them. The builders took every advantage of each site. Where the cave was high, the pueblo might rise to a height of three or even four stories at the rear, but elsewhere in the cave the buildings might be only a single story high. The walls did not have to be thick, for they could be braced against the cave ceilings, and in any case the pueblos were smaller than those of the mesa-top. The rooms were like jail cells: six by eight feet was a common size, and many ceilings were only four or five feet high. Doorways were about two feet high and sixteen inches wide. These cliffside pueblos had no space for luxurious sprawl.

Each cliff-house had an open plaza in front of the dwellings. It might be no more than twenty feet wide and a hundred feet long, but it was the center of the city's life. All day long the cliff-dwellers carried on their activities in the plaza and on the flat rooftops of the frontmost houses, retiring to their tiny rooms only when night fell. Though the rooms were cramped, their occupants made some attempt to decorate them, plastering their walls and often adding designs in red, yellow, white, and black paint. The kivas, too, were attractively decorated. They were located in the plazas. Because of the limitations of space, the cliff kivas had to be small, generally about a dozen feet across. But each cliff-house had many kivas, painstakingly excavated out of the cave floor. The biggest of the cliff-dwellings had twenty-three kivas. They followed the traditional pattern, with their fire-pits, smoke-holes, ventilator shafts, deflectors, and sipapus.

There was no place to farm on the side of a cliff, of course. The men of Mesa Verde still had to make their way to the fields on top of the mesas. The pueblo water supply, also, came from far away. Only a few lucky cliff-houses had water nearby. One actually had a spring bubbling out of the rear wall of the cave, but it was an exception. Usually the women of the pueblo had to make frequent journeys to springs on top of the mesas or in the bottoms of the canyons. Carrying five-gallon water jugs balanced on their heads, they scrambled skillfully up and down toe-holds cut in the face of the cliff.

When death came, it meant another journey away from the cliff. Since the cliff-houses were built on shelves of solid rock, it was impractical to bury the dead under the floors of rooms, as had sometimes been done in other Anasazi settlements. Nor was there space to bury the dead in the refuse heaps. A few burials were held there, archaeologists have discovered, but not many. The trash of the cliff-dwellings piled up in two places: against the rear wall of the cave behind the last row of rooms, and on the slope of the cliff below the pueblo. But only a handful of bodies have been recovered from such places.

One way of disposing of the dead was through cremation. This was practiced by the Hohokam, who burned their dead and often buried the ashes in handsome jars. Cremation has never been a common practice among the Pueblos, but apparently some of the dead were burned at Mesa Verde. J. W. Fewkes, an archaeologist working at the Cliff Palace ruin, reported in 1911 that one room was found to contain bushels of fine ashes and some burned human bones, along with the sort of gifts usually found with the dead. But cremation does not seem to have been widely practiced, and archaeologists today are still not sure where the Mesa Verde cemeteries, if there were any, are located. This is a puzzle at Chaco Canyon also. Pueblo Bonito, which was occupied for some 250 years, probably had an over-all population of nearly 6,000 during that time, but less than a hundred burials have been found there. The archaeologists hope that one day they will be lucky enough to discover the graveyards of Chaco Canyon and Mesa Verde, which will answer many questions about the Anasazi and perhaps yield a wealth of archaeological treasure.

The cliff-houses of Mesa Verde were inhabited for only a few generations. In one brief furious century of building, scores of the lofty, romantic dwellings were constructed, and then were abandoned. Nearly every canyon wall had its cliff-houses: great cities like Cliff Palace and Spruce Tree House, or small buildings inhabited by a single clan or even a single family. No doubt relationships were friendly among all these pueblos, and there was a good deal of visiting back and forth. Within a mile of Cliff Palace are thirty other cliff-houses, and probably the people of these neighboring pueblos regarded it as "the big city," visiting it just as small-town folk come to New York or Chicago today. There must have been trade between the pueblos too; one village may have had a man who was an expert axe-maker, another a man who excelled in weaving cotton blankets, a third village a celebrated jeweler, a fourth a first-class maker of arrowheads. We can picture a steady flow of traffic along the cliffside trails.

On the mesa-top, across the canyon from Cliff Palace, a strange building was erected late in the century. It is called Sun Temple today, because we think it was some kind of ceremonial structure. It is a D-shaped building with double-thickness walls twelve feet high, and does not seem ever to have had a roof or to have been inhabited. There is a central plaza surrounded by a maze of rooms, including several that may have been kivas. Perhaps Sun Temple was related to the Tri-wall at Aztec in some way—the shrine of a new religious movement that swept through the Anasazi during the fateful thirteenth century. The mystery of Sun Temple may never be solved.

It is linked to another and greater mystery: the wholesale abandonment of Mesa Verde. Not many years after Sun Temple's walls were constructed, the cliff-dwellers began to depart. They went away a few at a time, but the movement outward was a steady one, and by 1300 A.D. hardly anyone remained. The Four Corners country, ancestral home of the Anasazi, was left behind, and the Old Ones headed south and east and west to new lands, new homes.

Why?

Drought is one answer. The tree-ring tale is grim: almost no rain at all from 1276 to 1299. Lean harvests, springs running dry, trees withering in the canyons, and always the mocking smile of the cloudless blue sky. An entire generation was born and came to adulthood without knowing a real downpour. Farming became a grueling battle against dryness. Water had to be rationed; women walked for miles now to bring water from the nearest spring. The weak, the feeble, could not stand the suffering and hardship. Animals fled to greener pastures, cutting the game supply. The crops shriveled. Even the wild nuts and berries were hard to find, and the women searched endlessly for new sources of food. In the kivas the old men chanted and danced, begging the gods to send rain, and no rain came.

But the people of Mesa Verde had known drought before, and it had not driven them from their homes. Why did they leave now? Was this drought so much more terrible than those of the past?

Perhaps wandering warlike tribes were invading Mesa Verde at the same time. The cliff-houses themselves were safe from attack, but nomads rampaging on the mesa-tops could cut the Anasazi off from their fields and springs. There is little sign of actual warfare in the Mesa Verde area. But possibly the combination of drought and frequent raids convinced family after family that the gods had withdrawn their blessing from Mesa Verde, and that it was time to seek new homes. For a full generation the outward flow continued. Finally there was no one left.

The same movement was under way elsewhere. We have already seen that Aztec was abandoned at the same time, late in the thirteenth century. Chaco Canyon had been desolate for more than a hundred years. The remaining great center of Anasazi life in the Four Corners, in the Kayenta area, was also deserted now.

The Kayenta region, west of Mesa Verde and Chaco Canyon, had been an Anasazi territory since Basketmaker days. It had followed the general cycle of development from pit-houses to small pueblos. In about the year 1200, many of the Kayenta people migrated southward, and those that remained moved into cliff-houses. Most of these were small, and their architecture does not compare with that of the Mesa Verde cliff-dwellings. But three were quite large.

The biggest bears the Navaho name of Keet Seel today. This sprawling city in an enormous open cliff was built between 1255 and 1284. Eleven miles away is Betatakin, or Hillside House, whose 150 rooms were constructed between 1260 and 1277 on the sloping floor of a great cave in a sheer 500-foot sandstone cliff. Some twenty miles to the west is Inscription House, with 75 rooms; it gets its name from the time-weathered scrawl of an unknown Spaniard who visited it about 1661.

One novelty of these Kayenta cliff-houses is the kiva design. Some of the kivas at Keet Seel are of the usual circular underground type, but the others—and all six of the Betatakin kivas—are square or rectangular above-ground structures which have the customary fire-pits and deflectors, but which have doors instead of ventilating shafts. Pottery found in these cliff-houses is both black-on-white and polychrome, whereas at Mesa Verde nearly all the pottery was black-on-white except for the corrugated gray cooking ware.

Another Arizona canyon favored by the cliff-dwellers was Canyon de Chelly, east of Kayenta. This is a strikingly beautiful canyon whose almost vertical red walls rise as high as a thousand feet, framing a wide, flat valley through which a stream runs in rainy weather. A number of cliff-houses perch precariously on ledges in Canyon de Chelly and its branch canyon, Canyon del Muerto. One of the biggest is White House Ruin, built between 1060 and 1275, and abandoned by 1300. Its walls, plastered with a pinkish mud, glitter brightly when the sun enters the canyon. Lieut. J. H. Simpson gave the ruin its present name on his visit in 1849.

Simpson was in the vanguard of an army of white explorers who entered Anasazi country during the nineteenth century. Dr. John S. Newberry, whose description of Aztec Ruins was quoted above, entered Mesa Verde ten years after Simpson, but only the geology appeared to interest him, and he did not notice any of the ruins. Those who did paid little heed to them; they were miners or cattlemen, or members of the Ute Indian tribe that had taken possession of Mesa Verde after the Anasazi left.

The Utes were unfriendly, warlike Indians who frequently descended on the farms and mining camps of the white men now moving into their territory. Despite the threat of Ute savagery, an exploring party of geologists and geographers sent by the United States Government ventured into Mesa Verde in 1874. They had heard rumors from miners and farmers about the ruins in the cliffsides. A photographer named W. H. Jackson found and took pictures of a small pueblo that he named Two-Story Cliff House. Prowling in the debris on the floors of the small dark rooms, the explorers found pottery, corncobs, stone axes, and other Indian remains.

Jackson was only four miles from Cliff Palace, but he did not discover it. Fourteen more years went by, and on a snowy December day in 1888 two cowboys wandered into Mesa Verde in search of some stray cattle. One was Richard Wetherill, the other his brother-in-law, Charley Mason. The Wetherill family had a large ranch at the foot of Mesa Verde. Richard Wetherill and his four brothers had grown up among the Utes, and they were practically the only white men trusted by those suspicious, hostile Indians. A friendly Ute chief named Acowitz told Richard Wetherill about the great cliff-dwellings, and as Wetherill and Charley Mason jogged across the mesa-top that December afternoon they kept their eyes sharp for discovery.

They rode through the thick forest of juniper and pinyon pine covering the mesa, and came to a clearing that looked out across a canyon. Wetherill gasped and pointed. Framed by the great arch of its cave, its outlines softened by a haze of falling snow, a city of stone lay before them.

It took several hours to find a trail around the canyon and down the cliff. At last the two men stepped out onto the wide ledge of the cave and found themselves in a ghostly pueblo like none they had seen before. The cave was full of houses piled helter-skelter on terrace after terrace. Here was a tower four stories high; there another, round and tapering toward the cave roof. The tiny rooms held corncobs, pots, and stone tools. Rats were nesting in the storage chambers; debris filled the kivas. Human skeletons lay scattered about.

They gave the ruin the name of Cliff Palace—a name more poetic than accurate, since the pueblo never was a palace, but a town with hundreds of inhabitants. The solitary grandeur of its site, though, makes the name seem appropriate. After exploring Cliff Palace, Wetherill and Mason went in search of other ruins, Mason going to the north, Wetherill to the west. A short ride brought Wetherill to a second cliff-house, not as big as Cliff Palace but in a better state of preservation. It later was named Spruce Tree House.

Night was falling now. Wetherill did not enter Spruce Tree House, but turned back and met Mason. They camped for the night, and tried to return to Spruce Tree in the morning. But they lost their way and landed on the rim of a different canyon—and below them was yet another cliff-house.

When they brought back news of their discoveries, the other Wetherill boys went to see this wonderland of ancient cities. John Wetherill and three friends camped at Cliff Palace for a month, cleaning out a kiva and using it as a shelter. They poked through the debris of the ruin and collected a large number of pots and utensils, as well as finding fourteen bodies in the refuse dump. The Wetherills sold their collection of Cliff Palace artifacts for $3,000, a small fortune in 1889, and went into the archaeology business on a full-time basis.

It was open season at the Mesa Verde ruins. The

Wetherills dug everywhere. Luckily they had some notion of archaeological methods and kept careful notes on their findings, so they were not mere plunderers disturbing and destroying knowledge. Other travelers came and were guided to the cliff-houses by the Wetherills. A typical visitor was F. H. Chapin, who unabashedly wrote in 1890, "We remained long, and ransacked the structure from one end to the other."

Chapin's description of Cliff Palace is a good one. He wrote, "Surely its discoverer had not overstated the beauty and magnitude of this strange ruin. There it was, occupying a great oval space under a grand cliff wonderful to behold, appearing like an immense ruined castle with dismantled towers. The stones in front were broken away, but behind them rose the walls of a second story; and in the rear of these, in under the dark cavern, stood the third tier of masonry. Still farther back in the gloomy recess, little houses rested on upper ledges."

Another visitor in those early days was Baron Gustav Nordenskiold, a young Swedish archaeologist. "Strange and indescribable is the impression on the traveler," he wrote, "when, after a long and tiring ride through the boundless, monotonous pinyon forest, he suddenly halts on the brink of the precipice, and in the opposite cliff beholds the ruins of the Cliff Palace. . . . With its round towers and high walls rising out of the heaps of stones deep in the mysterious twilight of the cavern, and defying in their sheltered site the ravages of time, it resembles at a distance an enchanted castle." Nordenskiold dug in many of the cliff-dwellings at Mesa Verde, and carried off an extensive collection of artifacts—which today has found a strange home in a museum in Finland.

Nordenskiold was impressed by the masonry at Cliff Palace, even though it is not as good as some of the work done in the last days at Chaco Canyon. "The stones," he wrote, "are carefully dressed and often laid in regular courses; the walls are perpendicular, sometimes leaning slightly inwards at the same angle all round the room—this being part of the design. All the corners form almost perfect right angles, when the surroundings have permitted the builders to observe this rule." He commented on the doorways, many of an unusual T-shaped design, with a wider opening at the upper end than at the lower. These T-shaped doorways have never been satisfactorily explained; all we can say is that they were part of the Mesa Verde style of architecture. They are found in the Mesa Verde additions at Aztec, and in a few of the buildings in Chaco Canyon.

The fine stonework at Cliff Palace suffered heavily at the hands of the early explorers. To get at inner rooms that might contain valuable artifacts, the "pot-hunters" simply knocked holes in the walls. They wrenched beams from the roofs and floors to use as firewood, so that many rooms collapsed and much information about Mesa Verde roof-construction was lost to archaeology. So profitable was the trade in Mesa Verde pottery that such men as Charley Mason went back again and again. Speaking of an expedition he made around the turn of the century, Mason said, "In spite of the fact that all of the cliff dwellings had been worked over two or three times, we succeeded in making a very good showing."

It took a long time for people to realize that the Mesa Verde ruins were as much a part of the American heritage as the White House in Washington or Independence Hall in Philadelphia, and that the entire nation was being victimized by the wholesale looting. During the administration of Theodore Roosevelt, many of the great Anasazi ruins came under government control, and in 1906 Congress set Mesa Verde aside as a national park. The cliff-dwellings became public property. Such archaeologists as Jesse W. Fewkes entered the park to collect whatever artifacts the pot-hunters had failed to find. Fewkes also began the program of stabilizing the ruins; he rebuilt the walls where the cowboy-archaeologists had knocked holes in them, covered the tops of the buildings with cement to prevent further collapse, and installed runways to carry off the rain water that was undermining the foundations of some of the cliff-houses.

Today many of the cliff-dwellings at Mesa Verde have been fully excavated and stabilized. Cliff Palace, the largest of them, is visited by thousands of people every summer. They clamber down a fenced stairway—no Indian toe-hold trails for them!—to see the 200 rooms and 23 kivas of this 300-foot-long cave city, which once housed some 400 people. Spruce Tree House, with 114 rooms and eight kivas, is probably the most popular attraction in the park, because it is only a short walk from the lodge where park visitors stay. Another favorite is Balcony House, on the far side of the same mesa that holds Cliff Palace. Balcony House is unique at Mesa Verde because it still preserves a fragile balcony of wood and brush that once served the occupants of a second-story room as a place where they could work and get fresh air.

Balcony House was the fortunate pueblo that had a spring in its back yard. During the great drought it must often have been visited by women of neighboring pueblos in hopes of borrowing a jug of water. If the thirsty neighbors ever became too troublesome, the people of Balcony House had no difficulty in keeping them away, because the only entrance to the pueblo was virtually invasion-proof. Anyone trying to enter Balcony House had to come down an almost vertical cliff, then pass through a crack in the cliff wall. This crack was only a yard wide and twenty-five feet long, but the Balcony House folk made things even more difficult by building stone walls to flank it, creating a passageway through which one had to crawl on hands and knees. A big rock in the middle of the tunnel further hindered anyone trying to enter. Above this tunnel was a lookout post where a Balcony House warrior could hide. He would have a clear shot at any enemy who came scrambling through the passageway. He could hold off an entire horde with ease. Visitors who come to Balcony House today mount ladders to reach the pueblo, but when they leave they must crawl through the ancient tunnel—an experience that no traveler soon forgets, especially the wide-hipped ones.

The ruins at Mesa Verde receive more visitors each year than any other Anasazi site. Though everyone is welcome—for the national parks are there to be enjoyed—the heavy traffic has created some maintenance problems for the park rangers. So many people come to Cliff Palace that it has been necessary to close off most of the rooms. Cliff Palace and Balcony House can now be visited only in the company of a ranger, though Spruce Tree is open to all. Less spectacular, but of great interest, is a loop-road drive that carries visitors through the entire sequence of Anasazi development from pit-house to large pueblo. And to divert some of the tourist traffic from

Cliff Palace, archaeologists began working in 1958 at nearby Wetherill Mesa, where cliff-dwellings as imposing as the Chapin Mesa houses had gone unexcavated. Five years of scientific work at such ruins as Long House, Mug House, and Step House were followed by the installation of paved roads and power-lines so that these unfamiliar but exciting pueblos could be opened to the public.

Archaeologists continue to work on Chapin Mesa also, where many ruins on the mesa-top have yet to be surveyed, and where excavation has not even been started. Important discoveries are still being made. In 1962, rangers planning a new campground on the mesa-top came upon a series of long depressions in the ground, each about six feet wide and eighteen inches long. Archaeologists hurried to the site and found half a mile of such ditches, forming a network that served as a water-collection system for twenty-five acres of hillside. The ditches fed the runoff of rain water into a storage basin big enough to hold half a million gallons. It was given the name of Mummy Lake—"because it has dried up," a ranger explains. A ditch from Mummy Lake carried water to Spruce Tree House, four miles away, and perhaps even to Cliff Palace, another mile and a half farther on.

The discovery of Mummy Lake helped to increase our understanding of Mesa Verde farming 900 years ago. The rangers, incidentally, built their new campground somewhere else.

THE GREAT TREK

THE MIGRATION had been going on for generations. Year after year the Anasazi had left their homes, family by family, clan by clan. First Chaco, then Aztec and Mesa Verde, Kayenta and Canyon de Chelly, all were abandoned. By 1300 the Anasazi were gone from the Four Corners.

We know that the long drought of 1276–99 was one cause of this great trek. We think that warlike invaders also helped to send the Anasazi in search of safer territory. But actually there had been a steady flow of migrants through the Southwest for centuries. Though nothing could seem more permanent than a solid, massive stone pueblo, the Anasazi had frequently left their homes and fields and migrated to new areas. Their journeys are evidenced by the presence of Anasazi potsherds far from their place of origin.

Thus Chaco Canyon was originally settled by emigrants from north of the San Juan. Thus Pueblo Bonito came to greatness under a second wave of southbound wanderers. Thus Aztec was built by Indians from Chaco, and later taken over by Mesa Verde folk. And thus Kin Kletso, with its T-shaped doorways and its turtle-shell compactness, came to be built by Mesa Verde people in Chaco Canyon.

One explanation for this footloose tendency has come not from archaeologists but from anthropologists and ethnologists—scientists who study the customs and ways of the Pueblo tribes of today. They think it is an error to picture the Anasazi city-dwellers as members of a large, unified group. They suggest that Cliff Palace or any other big pueblo was actually a cluster of several independent towns. If the Anasazi society was organized the way the Pueblos are organized today—and that seems likely—then each big pueblo represented a conglomeration of several clans that had come together for mutual benefit.

The old unit-houses, with their ten or twenty rooms, probably were the basic pueblo group. The people of several unit-houses might combine to build a Chettro Ketl or an Aztec, because they could all live more comfortably if many people shared the work of defense, irrigation, and house repair. But each small clan group continued to worship in its own kiva, to maintain its own identity, to practice its own customs. No sense of a large community developed. In such a society there could easily be friction between one sub-group and another, and if the quarrels grew heated, an entire clan might pack up and move out. The great cities of the Classic Pueblo period may simply have disintegrated through feuding between clan and clan.

One group of Anasazi came down into central Arizona long before the breakup of the Four Corners society.

They began to arrive in 1064, the tree-ring experts say. Some time after September of that year, a volcano sprang from nowhere and showered fine ash over the region east of the present-day city of Flagstaff. All life perished as the smothering blanket of volcanic ash fell. But such ash is fertile for planting, and once the smoke had cleared the 800 square miles of cinder-covered land became first-class farm acreage.

An Anasazi branch moved down from its home in east-central Arizona in great numbers. But two other groups of Indians already dwelt in the vicinity. South of the volcano area, in the Verde Valley region, lived tribes of Hohokam, and on the plateau and forested foothills above the valley were Indians whom we call the *Sinagua,* a Spanish name meaning "without water."

The Sinagua, like the Hohokam and the Anasazi, were farmers. As their name implies, they were skilled at getting the most out of an annual sprinkling of rainfall; in their dry hills they managed to raise corn, beans, and squash, building diversion dams to trap what little rainfall and creek water they had. Their customs were not very different from those of the Hohokam. They lived in pit-houses made of poles, brush, and mud, but dug them deeper into the ground than did the Hohokam. They made polished brown pottery somewhat in the Mogollon style, and cremated their dead in Hohokam fashion.

When the volcano erupted in 1064, many of the Verde Valley Hohokam moved northeast to take advantage of the new fertility of the ash-covered region. The Sinagua promptly left their hills and replaced the Hohokam in the Verde Valley. In time they too headed for the volcanic area. By 1125, Hohokam, Sinagua, and Anasazi all were mingling in the Flagstaff vicinity.

The Hohokam and the Sinagua quickly came under the influence of these Anasazi, who are known as the Salado people after the place where they had previously lived. The three groups mixed in friendly fashion, and very shortly the pit-dwelling Hohokam and Sinagua were building above-ground stone pueblos in the Anasazi manner. The pueblo-building idea spread back into the Verde Valley, and hundreds of villages were constructed. The largest of these Sinagua-Salado pueblos in the cinder zone was Wupatki (a Hopi word meaning "tall house"), three stories high, with more than a hundred rooms. A short distance from the pueblo are the remains of a masonry ball-court, an indication of the strong Hohokam influence in the area.

Waves of Anasazi migration continued. The Sinagua were wholly absorbed in the Salado culture. The Salado people continued to press southward, into what had long been the heartland of the Hohokam. By 1200 drought began to afflict the Anasazi land—the first hint of the great drought of 1276–99—and the people who had entered the volcanic area around Flagstaff in 1065 now looked for river land to the south.

The Salado people began to build cliff-houses in the Verde Valley in the middle of the thirteenth century, at the same time as their cousins at Mesa Verde were building Cliff Palace, Spruce Tree House, and the rest. The most famous Verde Valley cliff-house is Montezuma Castle, a four-story building of seventeen rooms, with a "basement" of two storerooms, all arrayed in terraces on a steep cliff. Just west of the Castle was a six-story building, not a cliff-house, but built against the base of the cliff. It had perhaps 40 rooms once, but was destroyed by fire centuries ago.

The Hohokam seemingly did not object at all to having the Salado people continue south and west into their territory. The archaeological record shows that the invasion was completely peaceful. The Salado moved into existing Hohokam villages but built houses in their traditional Anasazi style. They cooperated with the Hohokam in maintaining the great irrigation canals, but each group continued to follow its own beliefs and customs.

The Hohokam had already begun to change their villages, perhaps under the influence of earlier Anasazi immigrants. Just before the Salado people arrived, the southern Hohokam had started to build villages that consisted of a dozen or more adjoining one-storied rooms, surrounded by a wall four or five feet high and seven or eight inches thick. Both the wall forming this rectangular compound and the houses within it were made of adobe reinforced by vertical posts.

The Salado, when they reached the hot, dry desert country of the Hohokam, wanted to build multi-storied pueblos of the kind their ancestors had erected. But Arizona's Gila Valley provided none of the useful, easily-worked sandstone of the north. The only building material was what the Hohokam were using: adobe.

So the Salado folk built skyscrapers out of mud. The best-known surviving pueblo of this period is the Casa Grande, or "Big House," midway between Phoenix and Tucson. A Jesuit missionary, Father Eusebio Kino, gave it that name when he discovered it in 1694, describing it as being "as large as a castle and equal to the largest church in these lands."

The Casa Grande is four stories high, dominating the desert. It is forty feet long, sixty feet wide; around it are lower buildings made up of large rectangular rooms. A thick wall that once may have been about eight feet high surrounds everything, making a compound 420 feet long and 230 feet wide.

This massive structure is built entirely of a reddish clay called caliche, found in the desert. Its Anasazi builders were obviously uneasy about constructing a high tower out of this material. They dug thirty-inch trenches for foundations, though foundations were not considered necessary in the north. Then they piled the clay up to form the walls, erecting courses about two feet high and letting them dry before adding new ones. When the walls of Casa Grande stood seven feet above ground level, the builders filled the rooms with earth, thus creating a seven-foot platform as a brace for their tower. Atop this they carried the caliche courses two more stories, and added a final central room on the fourth level. They built eleven rooms in all, each large enough to accommodate an entire Anasazi family comfortably.

The Casa Grande was built about 1300 A.D. By that time the entire Four Corners area had been abandoned, and more and more Anasazi were coming south. In the Gila Valley, Salado and Hohokam lived in their adobe villages, the Hohokam cremating their dead, the Salado-Anasazi burying theirs; the Hohokam constructing one-story houses, the Salado building towers. There are few comparable instances of two peoples with differing customs, backgrounds, and traditions living in such close harmony.

The period of cooperation lasted well over a century. Then, about 1400 or 1450, the Salado felt the old Anasazi urge to migrate once more. Why the Hohokam-Salado communities broke up is another mystery of the Southwestern past. Possibly friction developed between the two civilizations; perhaps the canal system began to fail, or the soil to lose its fertility. The warlike Apache Indians may have entered the area about this time. In any event, the Salado departed; the Hohokam, it is thought, stayed where they were, but went back to a simpler way of life, returning to pit-houses covered by shelters of brush. The modern-day Pima and Papago Indians are believed to be the descendants of these backsliding Hohokam.

WHILE THE SALADO BRANCH of the Anasazi was infiltrating Hohokam country, a general migration of the entire culture was under way elsewhere. With Mesa Verde and Kayenta deserted after 1300, a new phase of Anasazi life began.

Archaeologists used to call this new era Pueblo IV. It was described as "the stage characterized by contraction of area occupied . . . and, in general, by decline from the preceding cultural peak." Frank Roberts followed this way of thinking when he renamed Pueblo IV the Regressive Pueblo period, covering the years from 1300 to 1700 A.D.

To regress is to go backwards, and it may seem at first glance that the Anasazi did indeed regress during those years. They left their vast cities and settled in much smaller towns that could scarcely equal the awesome size of Pueblo Bonito or the airy grace of Cliff Palace. The new land they occupied was only a fraction of the size of their old territory. The curve of progress that had risen so steeply through the Developmental Pueblo days of 750–1050 and the Great Pueblo phase of 1050–1300 seemed now to swing sharply down.

Yet the so-called Regressive Pueblo period was actually a time of vitality and advancement. Archaeological work carried out since Dr. Roberts drew up his categories in 1935 shows a time of new experiments, of cultural evolution, that would make the name of Pueblo Renaissance more appropriate than that of Regressive Pueblo. Some archaeologists have come to use that term; others still employ the Roberts designation, though they agree that the period was not really regressive at all.

The wandering Anasazi went in many directions. The builders of Betatakin and Keet Seel and the other cliff-houses around Kayenta moved fifty or sixty miles south, to Antelope Mesa and Black Mesa. This was sandy, desertlike country, but there were springs trickling from the rocky cliffs, and the Anasazi did not demand a great deal of water to be happy.

Others kept heading south, across the eerie Painted Desert into the Petrified Forest, where trees many millions of years old had been transformed by slow chemical witchcraft into stone of many colors. They built a good-sized pueblo near the north end of the forest. Nearby is a boulder called Newspaper Rock, on which hundreds of petroglyphs were cut. At the south end of the forest is a much smaller pueblo of only a couple of rooms, which is one of the most amazing in the entire Southwest. It was built entirely out of chunks of petrified wood. Standing by itself on a low ridge overlooking the badlands of Arizona, this little pueblo seems like a dream-distorted version of the prosaic stone ruins of the Four Corners. The rough, unevenly-set blocks that form its walls glow with a dark radiance, with the shimmering reds and greens and violets of eternities-old petrified wood.

The pueblo outposts in central and southern Arizona did not last. About 1400 these Anasazi began coming north again. So, too, did the descendants of the old Sinagua people, who had been living in the Verde Valley for centuries, and the Salado folk who had gone on into the Gila Valley of the Hohokam. Those who returned from the south seem to have gone to the Antelope Mesa area of northeastern Arizona, where the Hopi pueblos were taking root.

The Hopi are an Anasazi group who have survived to our time with much of their ancient culture intact. In their own language, they are the *Hopitu*—"Peaceful Ones." The Spanish called them the Moqui, and they were known by that name until the beginning of this century. They settled on a group of rocky mesas about six hundred feet high, jutting southward into the flat desert like the fingers of a huge hand. The three Hopi-occupied mesas are actually limbs of a single great formation, Black Mesa.

The town of Oraibi on Third Mesa is the westernmost Hopi settlement, and probably the oldest. Dr. A. E. Douglass found tree-ring evidence that Oraibi had been settled at least as early as 1370. Archaeologists believe that the first Hopi may have arrived there about 1150. Two other ancient pueblos are on Second Mesa: Shungopovi and Mishongnovi, which were founded about 1250. Unlike Oraibi, these Second Mesa towns are not on their original sites. At first they were located in the foothills at the base of the mesa, and they moved to the top of the mesa about 1700. A third pueblo on Second Mesa, Shipaulovi, was settled about 1700 by residents moving from Shungopovi. The three present First Mesa towns, Walpi, Sichomovi, and Hano, were also built about 1700, though an older Walpi, on a terrace below the town of today, dated from 1300. There were other Hopi pueblos on nearby mesas, such as Awatobi on Antelope Mesa, but these have been abandoned in recent centuries.

The Hopi pueblos were built of stone covered with adobe plaster. Some of them occupied as much as ten or twelve acres of ground. The houses were arranged in long rows with wide plazas between them. In these plazas the Hopi built their kivas, using a radical new design that shows the adventurousness of the so-called "regressive" Anasazi. Their kivas were rectangular, twelve to fourteen square feet, each with a bench at one end. The floors were paved with blocks of sandstone, and contained the customary kiva features—sipapu, fire-pit, and deflector.

Another Hopi novelty was the use of coal. The Hopi mined soft coal and used it to heat some houses. To carry off the fumes, small chimneys sometimes were built. The Hopi were the only Indians of prehistoric North America to use chimneys and coal.

They were innovators in the art of pottery as well. The black-on-white and corrugated styles of pottery had gone out of fashion with the abandonment of the Four Corners region. Polychrome ware had made its appearance at Kayenta and other places in the Great Pueblo era. The first polychrome pottery was covered with an orange-red slip, on which a design was painted in black on the inner side of the bowl, in white on the outside. Later in the Great Pueblo period, the artists learned how to use all three colors on the same side.

The Hopi made black-on-yellow or black-on-cream pottery at first, but by 1400 they had begun to make outstanding polychrome-on-cream ware. The beautiful patterns in red and black paint on the light background are as striking as any ever produced in the pueblos. Hopi black-on-yellow took on an experimental character too; the artists splattered black paint over the yellow backgrounds to produce an effective stippled appearance. In time these Hopi pottery techniques fell into neglect and Hopi pottery became crude and unattractive. But early in this century archaeologists began to unearth the lovely ancient ware. A First Mesa woman named Nampeyo revived the old designs and brought about a rebirth of Hopi pottery, just as two potters at Acoma had revived the Mimbres styles. Today many women of the Hopi pueblos make pottery in the old manner for sale to tourists.

While the Hopi towns were being founded, other Anasazi were building big pueblos several hundred miles to the east. One new Anasazi colony took root just east of what is now the Arizona-New Mexico border. Many towns were built here. Six or seven were inhabited when Esteban and Fray Marcos de Niza arrived in 1539. These were the Seven Cities of Cibola, whose mud-plastered stone walls looked so sadly disappointing to Coronado's gold-seeking men. Probably the biggest of these pueblos was Hawikuh, which Coronado conquered. Today Hawikuh and the other cities of Cibola are in ruins, but the Indians still maintain one pueblo, Zuni. It was built about 1695 on the site of an older town, Halona.

The Zuni houses and kivas were much like those of the Hopi. One innovation in pottery originated among the Zuni: the use of a glaze made by mixing lead in the paint. Pottery decorated with this paint took on a gloss when fired. The Zuni made glazed ware in two types, a purplish-black-on-white and a dark-green-on-white. The glaze was difficult to apply and it was a long time before the artistic results were satisfactory. Eventually the idea spread to many of the other new pueblos.

Acoma, east of Zuni, was another of these new ones. This mesa-top pueblo was inhabited when Coronado reached it in 1540, and distinguished itself by its fierce resistance to Oñate some sixty years later. It may have been settled about 1300 by refugees from Mesa Verde. Acoma was an impregnable fortress for centuries. The only access to it was by a steep trail cut in the side of the mesa. Today, however, a road has been built, wide enough to permit automobiles to drive to the top. It is a narrow bumpy road that rises at an improbably steep angle, and not every car is powerful enough to make the ascent, but at least a road does exist.

A few miles from Acoma is another mesa which also

rises in sudden dramatic steepness from the flat desert. This is Mesa Encantada, the Enchanted Mesa, and an Acoman legend says that once it, too, was inhabited. The only way to reach the top was by climbing steps cut into a tall pillar of stone that leaned against the mesa. One day, so the story goes, the entire population was at work in the fields below the mesa, except for three women who had remained behind. One was sick, the other two were caring for her. An earthquake shook the mesa; the pillar of stone was shattered. Now there was no way to return to the mesa-top pueblo. The women stranded on the top perished, and the people of the Enchanted Mesa found new homes at Acoma. They had angered the gods in some way, and the gods had cast them from their pueblo.

Hundreds of years passed before anyone managed to climb the Enchanted Mesa to see if the story was true. Finally, about 1890, an ethnologist named Hodge found a way to the top and discovered that there really was a ruined pueblo there. Since then a path has been built and curiosity-seekers now often make the climb to the deserted pueblo.

The greatest concentration of Anasazi during the period following the exodus from the Four Corners lay farther to the east, along the course of the Rio Grande. A few Anasazi had lived there since Developmental Pueblo or perhaps even Modified Basketmaker days, but their villages had been isolated frontier outposts, never of any importance. Now, suddenly, the most advanced Anasazi of the north arrived and began to build pueblos. Probably the majority of the Mesa Verde people came here.

Scores of new pueblos were built along a zone several hundred miles long, from Taos in the north to a point close to the Mexican border. Castañeda, accompanying Coronado in 1540, counted some seventy different pueblos. Dozens more had been built and abandoned in the 240 years between the first wave of Anasazi settlers and the arrival of the Spaniards.

One pueblo that had run its entire course in those years was located in the canyon of the Rito de los Frijoles, or "Bean Creek," northwest of modern Santa Fe. This canyon cuts through the Pajarito Plateau, where many ruined pueblos have been found. Anasazi evidently had begun settling the region late in the twelfth century, and started constructing large pueblos by the fourteenth. They used an unusual building material here, since no sandstone was available. A great volcano had erupted, perhaps a million years ago, covering many square miles with ash. The volcanic ash had compacted into the soft rock known as *tuff*, and the Anasazi had built their pueblo out of blocks of this easily-worked substance.

The Frijoles Canyon pueblo is known as Tyuonyi. This means "meeting place" or "place of treaty" in the Keresan language, which is spoken in the nearby inhabited pueblos today. We do not know what name the people of Tyuonyi had for their pueblo. It was a sizable village, three stories high in some places, with about four hundred rooms, arranged in circular rows around a large central plaza. Many of the rooms are so small that it is hard to believe they were occupied by full-sized human beings. Probably the ground-floor rooms of Tyuonyi were used only for storage. The archaeologists who excavated them found that few of these rooms had fireplaces, which meant that they would have been uninhabitable in winter weather. Lacking chimneys, the pueblo-builders could have lighted fires only in upper-story rooms, since fires built in a lower story would have filled the rooms above it with smoke.

Tyuonyi was built between 1383 and 1513. Although it lies in an exposed place in a wide canyon, its builders made themselves secure against enemies by closing the entire pueblo but for one entrance into the central plaza. They drove stakes in zigzag pattern across the floor of the entrance area so that any attackers would be slowed if they tried to break in. Some of the Indians, apparently, did not care to live in the canyon-floor pueblo, for they built homes against the canyon wall nearby. These evidently were inhabited at the same time as Tyuonyi. Some of the houses were located at the foot of the cliff, but others were placed in caves higher in the rock.

The Frijoles Canyon cave-dwellings were not at all like the cliff-houses of Mesa Verde. Here, the Anasazi hollowed out small single-room dwellings, using stone tools to enlarge openings made by natural erosion. Hundreds of these cave-rooms lined the canyon for more than a mile. A typical room was about six feet by nine feet in size, with the ceiling five or six feet high. The doorways were small, three feet high and half as wide, to keep out the wind and rain. The floor and walls were plastered with mud. Since most of the rooms had fire-pits, soot generally covered the ceiling. Small openings in the front wall of the room allowed the smoke to escape. Five or six people might live in such a tiny room; though, as in all pueblos, the inhabitants spent as little time as possible in their homes.

The cave-dwellers also carved kivas out of the cliff. The cave-kivas of Frijoles Canyon are unique in Anasazi territory. They are oval chambers, some of them nearly twenty feet in diameter, with mud-plastered walls covered with soot. In the walls of the cave-kivas can be seen holes where beams once were set. These were supports for looms; here, as elsewhere, the men did their weaving in the kivas.

Tyuonyi and the adjoining cave-dwellings apparently went unnoticed by the Spaniards. The Frijoles Canyon region was abandoned in the sixteenth century, and its inhabitants moved eastward and southward. The present-day pueblos of San Ildefonso and Cochiti have legends that tell of a migration from the ruined villages of the Pajarito Plateau.

The southward thrust of the Anasazi continued all during the fourteenth, fifteenth, and sixteenth centuries. Many sites were inhabited no more than fifty years. Since building a pueblo was slow work, a village often was abandoned only a few years after it was completed. It is hard to account for this restlessness. A Hopi legend, which has its counterpart in stories told in the pueblos of the Rio Grande, says that the wanderings of the Anasazi were part of a divine plan to purify the people. Just as the God of Moses sent the Israelites to wander in the desert before entering the Promised Land, so, too, did the Anasazi gods require their people to go from place to place.

The legend tells how the Anasazi emerged into this

world from an earlier home somewhere below the surface of the earth. They came up through "the navel of the world," which is symbolized by the sipapu in the kiva. A guardian spirit named Masaw met them and explained that they would have to wander for many generations, following a predestined route, before they could take permanent homes.

Masaw gave each clan a small water jar. In many places along their journey, he said, they would come to desert regions. They were to plant the jar in the ground, and for as long as they remained, water would flow from it. "One certain person," said Masaw, "must be ordained to carry this water jar for the whole clan. He must be a holy person whose life is perfect in every way. Four days before you are ready to move on, this water-carrier must go without salt and he must pray. Then he will carry the jar until you arrive at the next stop on your migrations. For four days more he will pray and fast and go without sleep before planting the jar again. Then again the water will start flowing, and he may take up his normal life."

The sacred jar, said Masaw, would produce water even when planted on a high mountain or in a sandy desert. "The time will come," he told the people, "when the villages you establish during your migrations will fall into ruins. Other people will wonder why they were built in inhospitable regions where no water is to be found for miles around. They will not know about this magic water jar, because they will not know of the power and the prayer behind it."

The Hopi ended their migration in forbidding desert

country. No doubt the sacred jars still flow for them. The Anasazi who came to the Rio Grande, however, entered more agreeable country. They settled along the Rio Grande and the smaller rivers that feed it, and built pueblos that grew to have hundreds of rooms. The Pueblo Indians of today live on or near sites that have been continuously inhabited for centuries.

Some pueblos of the Rio Grande passed their peak of greatness early, and did not last. When Coronado arrived, the biggest and strongest was the easternmost pueblo, Pecos, at the headwaters of the Pecos River. It had a population of thousands, living in a rectangular four-story terraced building with smaller towns surrounding it. But because it lay so far to the east, it was subject to raids by the warlike Comanche Indians of the plains, and by 1750 the people of Pecos numbered less than a thousand. Although Pueblo Indians have never been good fighters, a war party set out from the pueblo about that time to meet the Comanche in direct combat. The expedition was ambushed and nearly all the young men of Pecos were slaughtered. A smallpox epidemic cut the population to a hundred and eighty in 1788, and thereafter the decline was so rapid that fifty years later only seventeen still lived in the huge pueblo. The people of Jemez, a pueblo eighty miles to the northwest and related in language to Pecos, invited the last survivors to live with them, and Pecos was abandoned forever.

Many other Rio Grande pueblos withered away as Pecos had done, but some flourished and endured. The Anasazi of this so-called "regressive" period multiplied in number, improved their farming techniques, and produced shining pottery of great beauty.

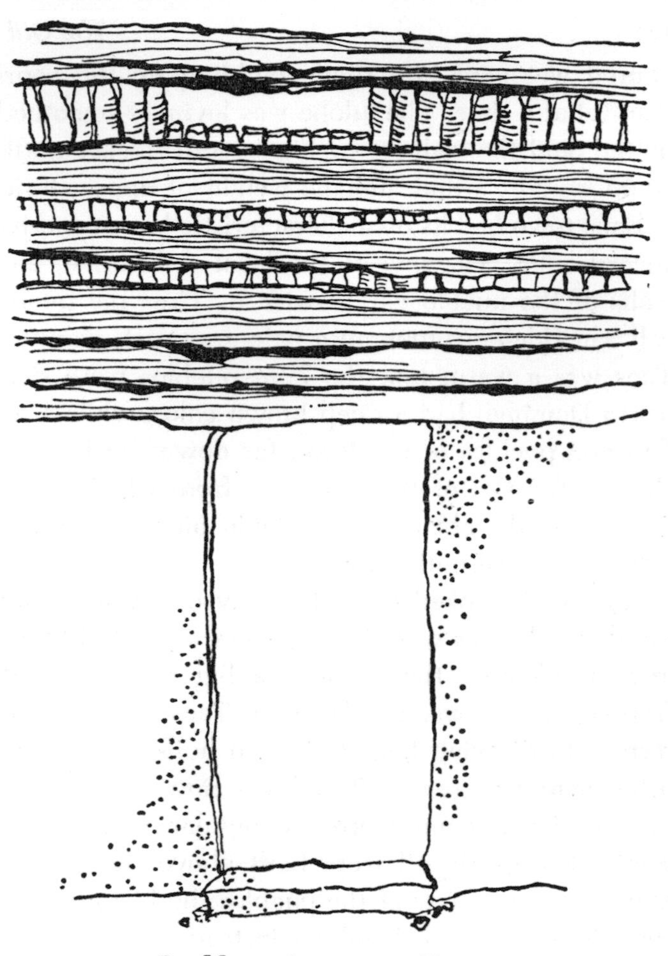

Pueblo roof structure, Taos

They were forced to learn new construction methods when they built their riverside pueblos. The sandstone of the north, so easily cut into flat slabs, was not available here. On the Pajarito Plateau, the Anasazi used blocks of volcanic tuff, but in the Rio Grande Valley they had to build with adobe. They set up frameworks of poles and poured wet mud into them, building up the courses a handful at a time. The adobe was lovingly smoothed and patted, and the walls grew higher and thicker until they could support a roof and the weight of upper stories.

Each town had its own characteristic layout and its own special color. The hue of the local soil varied, and the walls of the pueblo varied with it. Thus the pueblo we call San Ildefonso took on a pale gray cast; many-storied Taos was a warm tan; the Zuni pueblos were rich red. Santo Domingo had a deep brown color, while the now-deserted pueblos of the Piros, far down the Rio Grande, showed the tint of the pink clay from which they were made, and the abandoned Abiquiu on the Chama River was a dusty vermilion tone.

No pueblo looked quite like any other. At Santo Domingo the houses were in long rows separated by streets; at San Ildefonso they formed a big rectangular design framing an enormous plaza; at Taos, terrace rose on terrace to dizzying heights in two buildings facing each other across a stream. The kivas now were of strange new designs: some were rectangular and some were round, but nearly all were built above the ground like houses, and at a few of the pueblos the kivas were thrust right into groups of dwellings instead of being set apart.

Anasazi life had changed in many ways since the Old Ones had left Mesa Verde and the other pueblos of the north. The changes, though, had all been on the surface. What did it matter if the kivas now were above the ground instead of below, or if the villages were built of adobe instead of stone? The really important things remained the same. The corn still grew. The gods still watched over the people. The ceremonies still were observed, the ancient rites that brought rain and a good harvest, that kept enemies away, and that introduced children to the obligations and responsibilities of adulthood. Fifteen or twenty centuries had passed since the Anasazi had lived in brush shelters and gathered wild nuts for food. Patiently, in their own time, they had developed a rich, complex civilization. The people were busy and happy. Life was good.

Then came strange events.

First came a black man, bespangled with jewels, bedecked with feathers and rattles. He carried with him the trophies of the wild menacing Indians who lived beyond Anasazi country. He talked of other men, white men, who would soon arrive to instruct the Old Ones in religious matters.

The black man was too lordly, too demanding, too brash. The Old Ones did not understand him, so they put him to death. The white men came, just as he had promised. They spoke of a new god, a god of peace and mercy. The Anasazi, who understood peace, listened with interest. But these Spaniards who preached peace practiced war. They stole food, they swaggered through the pueblos like masters, they peered into the kivas without seeming even to realize that they were sacred. And they demanded gold. There was no gold in Anasazi country. The people of the pueblos had never used any metal at all, not even bronze or copper or iron. They certainly had no use for the soft, shiny, yellowish stuff that the white men prized so highly.

It was not the fault of the Pueblos that they had no

gold, but the Spaniards did not seem to understand that. They grew angry, threatened, blustered, put chains on the important men of the pueblos. The people came to realize that these Spaniards, for all their talk of a god of mercy and justice, were enemies who must be driven out. There was war; Spaniards died, but many more perished on the other side. At last the strange ones left, exhausted by their own long fruitless quest for yellow metal.

The Pueblos shrugged and returned to their fields. Spring, summer, fall, winter, year followed year—and the white men returned. They came a few at a time at first, talking of their god. The Pueblos killed them quickly: it was the simplest thing to do. But then came an army. The white man named Oñate announced that he now ruled all this land in the name of a king who was far away, and in the name of a god with soft eyes and a long beard. It did not seem practical to fight this man. How could farmers with arrows and clubs defeat men in gleaming armor who wielded swords and carried rifles that could kill with a voice like thunder?

Acoma tried to fight, and Acoma met flaming destruction. The other pueblos surrendered, and the white men began to build a city.

Things had changed in Anasazi-land, and they would never again be the same.

AFTER THE CONQUEST

WITH OÑATE'S ARRIVAL, the Spaniards had come to stay. Oñate himself was recalled by King Philip III in 1606, and after fighting the order for a few years he left New Mexico forever. But the new governor founded the town of Santa Fe in 1610, replacing Oñate's short-lived capital of San Gabriel, and the Spanish grip on the Pueblos grew firmer.

The Spaniards no longer denied that it was folly to think of finding gold in New Mexico. A different treasure excited them: souls. The Spaniards vowed to turn the Indians into good Christians, even if they had to be killed by the wagonload in the process. Twenty-six friars spread out through the pueblos, and by 1625 some fifty churches had been built. Even high Acoma was given a church. Its people hauled heavy logs to the summit of the mesa to build a magnificent house for the god of the Spaniards.

The pueblos were given new names, the names of saints. The names most of the villages bear today, such as Santa Clara, San Ildefonso, Santo Domingo, and San Juan, are names bestowed by the priests. The people themselves preserved the old names of their pueblos, just as they continued to call themselves by Indian names even after the padres baptized them with proper Spanish ones like Juan Padilla and Gregorio Herrera. The priests even taught the Indians how to build better pueblos. Houses built of shapeless lumps of clay quickly melted in the rain, and needed constant repair. The Spanish priests showed the Pueblos how to make bricks by mixing straw with wet clay and pressing the raw material into wooden molds ten by eighteen by five inches. The bricks were allowed to dry in the sun; then they could be used to build neat, regular walls.

There was no room for pagan rituals in the kingdom of Christ. The Spanish clergy fought hard to stamp out the old religion. Kivas were burned, and masks and sacred images were thrown on the fires. The medicine men and elders of the pueblos were branded as witches; many were whipped into submission, and the stubborn ones were executed. The Indians were forced to attend church services and to support and feed the Catholic priests.

While the missionaries flogged and hanged the Pueblos to save their souls, the civil authorities were equally severe. The Spanish governors named cooperative Indians as local officials, ignoring the traditional village structure of government. They insisted that Indians be tried in Spanish courts, under Spanish law that was incomprehensible to them. High-spirited *caballeros* spurred their horses through Pueblo cornfields, not caring about the destruction of the crops. The Indians were virtually turned into the slaves of the Spanish.

There were revolts. The gentle Pueblos were forced to

strike back at their masters. Spanish priests had arrived at the Hopi pueblo of Awatobi in 1629 and made many converts, but within four years one of the fathers was martyred. At Oraibi the people were compelled to carry logs from a forest forty miles away to build the huge mission. They called it "the slave church," and felt despair when the neglected Anasazi gods refused to send rain to the converted people. Drought bred famine; many Hopi perished, others migrated to the Rio Grande. About 1645 there was an uprising at Jemez Pueblo, and a Spaniard named Naranjo was killed; in return the local governor hanged 29 Indians and imprisoned many more as "witches." Other rebellions broke out, but were quickly put down.

The Spaniards, knowing they lived in constant danger, saw sorcery everywhere. In 1675 a missionary became convinced that some of the Spanish colonists had been bewitched. He accused many Indians, and forty-seven were convicted of witchcraft. Four were hanged, the rest whipped.

Slowly the fires of revolt grew hotter in these peaceful people. They numbered ten times as many as the 2,400 Spaniards in New Mexico, but they lacked leadership. What they needed was someone who could rally the men of the scattered pueblos and lead them in attacking the hated oppressors.

The leader appeared. He was Popé, a medicine man of the pueblo called San Juan. Popé was one of the forty-three so-called witches whipped and imprisoned in 1675, and when the Spaniards released him, a bitter, hatred-filled old man, he took refuge in the large pueblo of Taos.

He hatched a plot and quietly won the allegiance of pueblo after pueblo, even to the far-off Hopi villages on their remote mesas. Only the pueblos farthest down the Rio Grande, Isleta and the Piro villages, did not join the alliance.

A knotted cord was the symbol of rebellion. It was planned that August 13, 1680, was to be the day on which every Indian rose against the Spaniards, and swift runners brought the knotted cords to each pueblo. The knots were a code, announcing the day of action. But on August 9, converted Christian Indians in several of the pueblos told their priests of the plot. Spanish messengers carried the warning to those in outlying areas, telling them to flee to Santa Fe for safety. With the plot revealed, Popé ordered an early attack. On the morning of August 10, men of Taos, Picuris, and several other northern pueblos struck before dawn. In the next few days pueblo after pueblo rose. The Indians attacked "with shamelessness and daring," wrote the Spanish governor.

Priests were butchered in their churches, and their bodies stacked on the altars. Those settlers who had not had time to escape were surrounded and slain. Four hundred Spaniards died, nearly a fifth of New Mexico's white population. The survivors, about two thousand of them, took refuge in Santa Fe.

They were attacked by an army of screaming, maddened Indians. The Santa Fe garrison, led by Governor Antonio Otermin, numbered only 150 able-bodied soldiers, but managed to hold the Indians off during a five-day siege. The church and convent were burned, the suburbs destroyed, the water supply cut off. A suicidal charge by the Spaniards turned the tide; three hundred Indians were killed and many wounded, at a cost of only five Spanish lives. The Pueblos withdrew to the nearby hills.

On August 21 Otermin decided to evacuate Santa Fe. A forlorn band of colonists headed south on foot, carrying whatever possessions they could. There were hardly enough horses for the sick and the wounded. The Indians watched, but did not attack. Under a fierce summer sun, the retreating Spaniards made their way past Santo Domingo Pueblo, where three priests and eight other Spaniards had died, then to the pueblos of San Felipe and Sandia, where the priests had escaped but the missions had been destroyed, and on to the friendly pueblo of Isleta. By the end of September the Spaniards had withdrawn entirely from New Mexico and were settled in the vicinity of what is now El Paso, Texas.

The Pueblos were their own masters again.

The kivas were rebuilt. Crosses and churches were burned. Images of Jesus, Mary, and the saints were gleefully fed to the flames. "The god of the Christians is dead," Popé proclaimed. "He was made of rotten wood." Popé decreed that nothing brought to New Mexico by the Spaniards should be kept, not even the plants they had introduced—watermelons, peaches, chilies, onions, wheat. The pigs and sheep of the colonists were slaughtered. The horses were released from the corrals. They were promptly captured by the fierce Indians of the plains, and an entire civilization was thereby transformed. The reckless, hard-riding Sioux and Kiowas and Shoshone and Cheyenne who thundered across the endless plains until the late nineteenth century were mounted on steeds descended from those set free in Santa Fe in 1680.

Popé went too far in his hatred of everything Spanish. He tried to make himself absolute dictator over all the Pueblos, which no man had ever attempted before. He garbed himself in a fantastic outfit of gaudy hue and wore a bull's horn on his forehead, and went from pueblo to pueblo, demanding to be received as a monarch. Those who opposed him were put to death. Taos and Pecos and several other river pueblos backed him; the rest broke away, crying that his rule was even more oppressive than that of the Spaniards. After a few short months of unity, the pueblos were set against each other in strife.

In the autumn of 1681, Governor Otermin attempted to reconquer New Mexico. He marched north with 146 soldiers and found that the pueblos of the Piros—Socorro, San Pascual, Alamillo, and several others—had been abandoned. Not till he reached Isleta, just south of present-day Albuquerque, did he find an inhabited pueblo. Isleta put up token resistance, but quickly surrendered. Its people had always been friendly to Christianity, but they had another and more urgent reason for submitting. They had had a good harvest, and their storage bins were full of corn. In the north, the quarrelling rebels were stricken with famine, and Isleta feared a raid by hungry men of the northern pueblos.

In December, Otermin journeyed up the Rio Grande. He stopped at the Tiguex pueblos, Alameda, Puaray, and Sandia, and found them deserted but well stocked with corn. He burned the granaries, and the towns themselves, to keep the food from falling into rebel hands.

A few days later, Otermin chose an officer named Dominguez to lead a small force northward on a reconnaissance mission. Dominguez came to the pueblos of Cochiti, San Felipe, and Santo Domingo, which were also abandoned. He was about to burn them, but decided against it when a rebel chief from Cochiti promised to bring about the surrender of all his fellow conspirators in a day and a half. Dominguez returned to Otermin and told him of the plan, but Otermin realized it had been nothing but a trick to gain time while the rebels gathered their forces. Heavy snow began to fall. Fearing to fight in winter on the home terrain of the Pueblos, Otermin withdrew. Soon after, he was replaced by a new governor.

The Pueblos remained undisturbed for years, fighting among themselves, but unchallenged by the Spaniards. The years of independence were hard ones. Popé was overthrown several times, but managed to restore his dictatorship. Drought struck, bringing famine. The wild nomads of the north and east invaded the pueblos, and now, on horseback, they were more deadly than ever.

At last came Don Diego de Vargas, named Governor and Captain-General of New Mexico in 1688. He was a tall man with long dark hair and a slender, pointed beard, and he was wealthy and self-assured, a born commander of men. From his headquarters at El Paso, Vargas led sorties that brought the Indians of northern Mexico and western Texas under control, and on August 21, 1692, he felt ready to begin the reconquest of New Mexico.

He found, as Otermin had found eleven years before, that all the southern pueblos had been destroyed and deserted. On September 13 he appeared at Santa Fe with less than a hundred soldiers. The former Spanish capital was occupied by Indians. They were fortified to withstand a siege, but Vargas talked them into surrendering. Apparently they had had enough of independence, after twelve years of drought, sickness, hunger, and civil war. Vargas took possession of the city. To him came Tupatu of Picuris Pueblo, the most powerful rebel chief since Popé's death a few years before. He offered his allegiance to Spain. With Tupatu at his side, Vargas toured all the northern pueblos. One after another they yielded without fighting. A thousand children born during the years of revolt were baptized.

By November, Vargas appeared at Acoma. It surrendered, as did Zuni, and there were more baptisms. He went on to the Hopi mesas, and was received coolly but without open hostility. Those that Vargas visited surrendered to him; he did not get to Oraibi at all. Satisfied with his work, he returned to El Paso just before Christmas.

At least in theory the Pueblos were pacified once more. But there were no Spanish garrisons in New Mexico, no colonists. The surrender was unreal. In October, 1693, Vargas gathered seventy families of colonists and a hundred soldiers and returned to Santa Fe. It was occupied by Indians again. This time, because the Spaniards had come to stay, the Indians had to be driven out by force. The siege lasted all day; arrows, stones, and boiling water showered down from the walls on the attackers. Vargas prevailed, and the rebels were imprisoned.

Now he repeated his journey of the year before, but the friendly submission of 1692 had changed to stony opposition. All through 1693 and 1694 and 1695 Vargas fought the Indians, conquering the pueblos one by one. Priests returned; the missions were rebuilt. But new rebellions flared constantly. Taos, Picuris, and the other northern pueblos massacred Spaniards in 1696, and the rebels fled to Acoma, Zuni, and the Hopi country. Vargas executed as many of them as he could capture. It was a time of great uncertainty in the pueblos. The people of one entire village abandoned it after slaying their Catholic missionary, and trekked hundreds of miles westward to First Mesa in Hopi country. Though they spoke a different language from the Hopi, and had somewhat different customs, they were welcomed and allowed to settle. The refugees founded the town of Hano, which they still occupy as a little pocket of Rio Grande people surrounded by Hopi.

Vargas, tireless and determined, eventually brought all the New Mexican pueblos under his control. By setting pueblo against pueblo, and displaying at all times his own unbending strength, he outlasted the many brief rebellions of 1693 to 1696. The Spaniards had learned a sober lesson from the long Pueblo uprising that had begun in 1680; they had learned that Christianity could not be forced upon the Indians. The new missionaries who entered New Mexico had to resign themselves to the fact that the kiva and the church would exist side by side.

The Hopi villages had officially submitted—all but Oraibi, which was never asked—but they remained aloof and independent. They were so far away that the Spaniards did not try to draw them into close control. In 1700, however, Padre Juan Garaycoechea visited Awatobi, the easternmost Hopi pueblo, and converted seventy-three Hopi to Christianity. When news of this reached the neighboring mesas, it stirred painful memories of the days seventy years before when Hopi had toiled to build "the slave church" for the white masters. Was that slavery to return? Men of Oraibi, Walpi, Shongopovi, and Mishongnovi met secretly to discuss the situation. It was late in October; in a few weeks it would be time to begin the annual cycle of religious ceremonies. It was intolerable to think that those ceremonies would have to be held while Hopi nearby sang the praises of the white man's god.

A solemn decision was reached. The men of the other Hopi pueblos decided that Awatobi must be destroyed, and one of the darkest episodes in Pueblo history followed.

The attack was sudden and silent. As dawn was breaking the Hopi men filed quietly to the top of Antelope Mesa. A man of Awatobi who opposed the return of Christianity opened the sturdy wooden door that was the only entrance to the pueblo. The attackers burst in. Many men of Awatobi had gathered in the kiva that night to prepare for the great festival, for they meant to keep the old ways even while adopting Christianity. A blazing torch was thrust into the kiva. Its roof burst into flames.

The invaders raced through the village, striking down men and boys, women and children. Only a few women and girls were spared—just those who had not been baptized, and who knew and could recite the prayers of their own clans. By the time the sun rose, Awatobi was thick with dead and dying. The surviving women were carried away to other pueblos. The attackers finished their task by despoiling the village itself, tearing down walls, smashing pottery, shattering looms. When night fell Awatobi was a smouldering ruin. It was never reoccupied. J. W. Fewkes, the archaeologist who dug there in 1892, found chilling evidence of the massacre. He wrote, "The earth was literally filled with bones, evidently hastily placed there or left where the dead fell. These bodies were not buried with pious care. . . . Many of the skulls were broken, some pierced with sharp implements." His Indian workmen were so horrified that he had to call a halt to the excavation.

The doom of Awatobi kept Christianity out of the Hopi pueblos for more than a hundred years thereafter. In 1776 a brave priest named Francisco Garcés came to Oraibi alone, and camped in the street. The Hopi ignored him. They would not even sell him food, and they would not listen to his talk of Jesus. After two days he was asked to leave. He accepted defeat and loaded his belongings on his mule. "Having arranged my things," he wrote, "I mounted on her back, showing by my smiling face how much I appreciated their pueblo and their fashions." The Hopi escorted him from the town. The day was July 4, 1776. Not only the Continental Congress in Philadelphia was showing independence on that day.

Later that year another priest, Fray Silvestre de Escalante, came to Hopi territory and met with the same cool defiance. He remained long enough to take a census, and reported a Hopi population of 7,494. Then drought and plague struck. No rain fell for three years. A Spanish expedition in 1780 found only 798 Hopi alive; in the last four years, nine out of every ten had died. Of 30,000 sheep, only 300 remained. There were five horses, no cattle.

The pueblos along the Rio Grande also knew hardship. There were five thousand deaths from smallpox in 1780 and 1781. Many of the pueblos became virtual ghost towns. Pecos was the hardest hit, but others suffered; the population of Zia dropped from 568 in 1760 to 275 in 1793, that of San Ildefonso from 484 to 225. Picuris, which had had a population of 3,000 before the revolt of 1680, had less than 200 as the eighteenth century neared its close.

There were other enemies beside famine and plague. For many centuries, scattered bands of nomads had bedeviled the Anasazi farmers. In some years the danger was greater than in others. Perhaps whole generations went by without serious attack, but during times of drought the nomads went on the warpath, raiding the well-stocked granaries of the prudent Anasazi; when times were easy, the wild ones went elsewhere. The drought era of 1276–99 was probably a time of steady nomad invasions, leading eventually to the wholesale evacuation of the Four Corners.

Now, in the late eighteenth century, the savage raiders were back. They had horses by this time and a name. They were the Navaho. Coronado made no mention of them in his report of 1540; Espejo said nothing about them, nor did Oñate. But Fray Escalante drew a map in 1776 that labeled the entire pueblo region the "*Provincia de Navajoo.*" And an official Spanish report of 1785 observed that "the Navaho nation has seven hundred families more or less, with four or five persons to each one."

The Navaho, and their cousins the Apache, had arrived. They came from the far north. The evidence of their northern origin lies in their language, which belongs to the Athabascan group of languages spoken by the Indians of western Canada and Alaska. The Navaho-Apache dialect is related to the dialects of the north closely enough to permit a Navaho of the Arizona plateau to carry on an understandable conversation with a caribou-hunting Indian of the Yukon, even though centuries have passed since the Navaho came south.

We do not know when the nomads of the north reached Anasazi country. Pottery of a kind made by certain Athabascan-speaking tribes has been found in Gobernador Canyon near Aztec, New Mexico, in association with tree-ring dates of 710–875 A.D. There is evidence of fire destruction at this settlement, so perhaps it was ransacked by an advance party of northern nomads. The identification is still unsure.

The next nomad invasion seems to have come about 1100 A.D. Archaeologists working in the Colorado Rockies have found circular stone buildings resembling the domed lodges, called *hogans,* that the Navaho build. And Athabascan-like pottery has been found—again associated with burned pueblos—at several minor Anasazi sites. One archaeologist has suggested that these nomads, who had forced the abandonment of the Gobernador region three centuries before, leaving pottery with pointed bottoms on the scene, "also caused Pueblo people in the adjoining area to move from small settlements and build the large pueblos in Chaco Canyon for their own protection."

We suspect that during the late years of the Great

Pueblo period—from about 1150 to 1300—the Anasazi were constantly harassed by these northern-born nomads. But the archaeological proof has not yet been found. The next definite sign of Athabascan invasion comes from the Gobernador Canyon area and dates from about 1500 A.D. A definitely Navaho-looking group of Indians occupied the area for almost three hundred years starting at about the time of the landing of Columbus. Archaeologists have found pointed-bottom pottery, and Navaho hogans of a familiar kind, built of logs, brush, and earth.

By the year 1600 there certainly were northerners roaming Anasazi country. They did not call themselves Navaho or Apache. Their name for themselves was Diné, "the People"—a word used as a tribal name by all Athabascan-speaking Indians. The pueblo-dwellers called them *apachu,* meaning "stranger" or "enemy." One band became known as *apachu nabahu,* "enemies of the cultivated fields." The Spanish translated these names into Apache and Navaho, and the names stuck so well that the Diné themselves have come to use them.

The invaders were not farmers. They were a wandering race of warriors, aggressive, shrewd, strong. They came from a cold land where they had had no tradition of farming, because the earth would not yield crops; here in the Southwest, they lacked the patience to struggle against drought as the hard-working Pueblo farmers did. It was easier to let the Pueblos do the farming, and then to burst in and carry off the harvest.

Nor did they care to build great cities out of stone or adobe, as the Pueblos did. The Navaho and Apache felt no need to settle down. They had no wish to live in groups that sometimes numbered several thousand, all jammed together in a village of tiny rooms. They liked privacy. They chose to travel in small family-sized bands and to live in lonely dwellings placed at great distances from one another. The Navaho built circular hogans of logs and brush, covered with mud. The Apache dwelling was a round hut of brush, the *wickiup*. Both nomad branches made crude pottery and fairly good baskets. They dressed in skins, and sometimes in garments woven of juniper fiber.

The Apache lived in the East, from southeastern Colorado and northern New Mexico as far east as Kansas, Oklahoma, and Texas. They lived by raiding, and never learned the arts of the more civilized Indians around them. But the Navaho proved to be swift learners. They took naturally to the raising of sheep, and became the best herders and stockmen of the Southwest. They even learned a little about farming, and raised peaches and corn in a hit-or-miss way in some of the Arizona canyons. From the Pueblos the Navaho borrowed the art of weaving, and in time came to excel at it. Though it was the men who did the weaving among the Pueblos, the women were the ones who mastered the loom among the Navaho, and their colorful blankets became an important trade item. The Navahos borrowed many religious ideas also from the Pueblos, combining the Pueblo rituals with their own beliefs.

Taller and stronger than most of their Pueblo neighbors, the lean, rangy Navaho throve at a time when the Pueblos seemed threatened with extinction. Navaho population doubled and doubled again. The harried people of the adobe villages found themselves surrounded by an ever-multiplying horde of fierce enemies. The Hopi called them the Tavasuh, "the Headpounders," because they killed captured enemies by hitting them with rocks or stone axes. Their raids grew more frequent as their numbers increased. In 1785 the Navaho were thought to number about three thousand; sixty years later they were estimated at seven to fourteen thousand, with ten thousand head of horses, mules, and donkeys, half a million sheep, and three thousand head of cattle. They were increasing at the expense of their peaceful neighbors. When the Navaho needed corn they took it from the nearest pueblo. Sheep, horses, slaves, jewelry, they stole at will.

The Pueblos tried to fight back, but they had no zest for fighting. They were a tired, discouraged, dwindling people, thinned by disease and by the long hopeless struggle against the Spanish. War had never been loved among the Pueblos. In other Indian societies war was the supreme test of manhood, thrilling and glorious. Not here. To a man of the pueblos war was an evil necessity, something that had to be endured reluctantly and sadly. When the time of war arrived, a man of the pueblos painted himself with war-paint, armed himself, asked for divine help. But the song he sang was never the gloating, bragging war-song of other Indian cultures. He might sing something heavy-hearted and fatalistic, like this:

So we have bad luck,
For we are men.
You have good luck,
For you are women.
To Navaho camps we go
Ready for war. Good-bye.

To Navaho camps they went, and often died. Those who returned victorious felt no sense of great accomplishment. If they had taken life, they had to be purified in special ceremonies before they were allowed to rejoin the community.

All during the first half of the nineteenth century the Navaho and Apache raids made life miserable for the Pueblos. In the old days the Anasazi would have abandoned their villages and moved on to new territory. That could no longer be done. For one thing, under Spanish rule the people of the pueblos were required to remain on their own land. They were no longer free to migrate. The best land, anyway, belonged to Spanish settlers. Where could the Pueblos go? They had to remain in their crumbling mud villages, which grew more desolate with each passing decade. Even migration could not have helped them, for the Navaho had horses, and could reach any village of the Pueblos, no matter how far they went.

But the Navaho and the Apache were also raiding the cities of the white men, and that was their downfall. Quiet Pueblo farmers could not fight back, but the white settlers could and did. And now a new breed of white man was coming into the Southwest.

Spain had lost her grip on the New World. In 1822 Mexico won her independence and the pueblos passed from Spanish to Mexican control. That in itself did not make much difference. But New Mexico was not destined to remain a Mexican province for long. The young adventurous United States of America was looking westward. Traders had opened the Santa Fe Trail, and furs, gold, and silver were traveling along it to the rich cities of the east. The United States talked of a "manifest destiny" to expand from coast to coast, and Mexico stood in the way.

In 1846 President Polk declared war against Mexico. The Mexican War is not the noblest episode in American history; it amounted to little more than a blunt grab of territory belonging to another country. But "manifest destiny" would not be denied. On August 18, 1846, General Stephen Watts Kearny entered Santa Fe and raised the American flag. Not a shot had been fired. The bloodless conquest was confirmed in 1848 by the Treaty of Guadalupe Hidalgo, in which Mexico was compelled to yield to the United States the vast territory now comprising the states of New Mexico, Arizona, Utah, Nevada, and California. In return, Mexico received the modest sum of $15,000,000.

The Pueblos now came under United States administration. They became the responsibility of the Bureau of Indian Affairs, part of the War Department. In March, 1849, the Department of the Interior was created, and the Bureau of Indian Affairs was transferred to it, so that civilians, and not soldiers, were given the task of dealing with the Indians.

There were no problems with the Pueblos: "a more upright and useful people are nowhere to be found," wrote the government agent at Santa Fe. But the Apache and Navaho remained very much a military problem. Although the Spanish and the Mexicans had been unable to control them, the United States set out to bring them to heel.

American troops marched into New Mexico and Arizona. The commanding officer tried to make treaties with the Navaho, but there was no central authority, only a number of completely independent bands. In 1851 Fort Defiance was established in Arizona as a military outpost designed to keep the wild ones under control. The friction mounted until 1858, when the Navaho launched a massed attack on the fort, and violence ruled the day.

The outbreak of the Civil War halted the effort to pacify the Navaho and Apache. In 1863 the scout Kit Carson was given the job of dealing with them. He cut down their peach orchards, butchered their herds of sheep and cows, destroyed their fields of corn. The Navaho took refuge in high-walled Canyon de Chelly, and Carson kept them hemmed up in there until they began to submit. Finally, thousands surrendered. They were marched hundreds of miles to the Bosque Redondo, a reservation in eastern New Mexico, and were confined there.

The government hoped to turn them into farmers. They were given seeds and tools and were shown how to plant crops. But though some of the Navaho had done a little farming, most were shepherds or warriors who regarded agriculture as hateful. The government was asking the Navaho to change the basic nature of their culture at the snap of a finger. It could not be done. Nomads cannot be turned into agriculturists overnight.

A golden stream of dollars was poured into the Bosque Redondo reservation, but none of the Navaho became farmers. In the first three years a few fields were planted; in the fourth there was no planting at all. The government

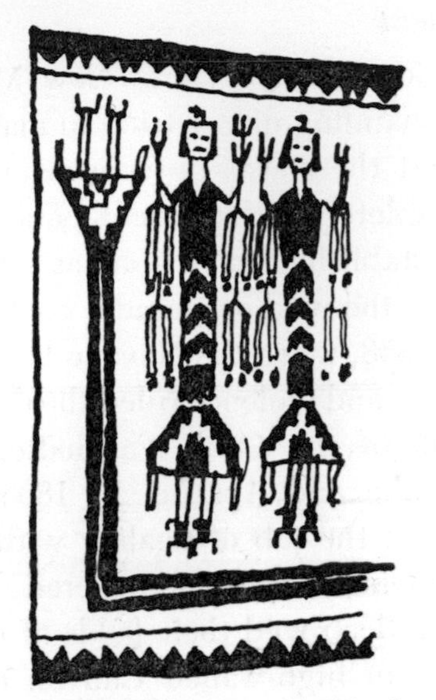

Detail from a Navaho blanket

sent General Sherman to investigate, and he reported that it would be cheaper to board the whole tribe at the Fifth Avenue Hotel in New York than to continue the experiment. "Let us go home," the Navaho begged him.

In 1868 they were allowed to leave. They were given a large reservation in northeastern Arizona upon their promise not to fight again. They have kept that promise. They planted small farms; they began to raise sheep and cattle once again; the women made blankets for sale, and the men began to fashion silver jewelry made from beaten-down Mexican silver coins. The massive silver ornaments, often decorated with turquoise inlays, became greatly popular among the Southwestern Indians, and soon the craft spread from the Navaho to the Pueblo tribes, notably the Zuni. By the beginning of the twentieth century, the Navaho were on the road to prosperity—and off the warpath forever.

The story of the Apache is not so cheerful. They, too, were subdued by American soldiers. They fought stubbornly for a full generation after their Navaho cousins had decided to cooperate with the white man. When they were finally rounded up, they were shifted from reservation to reservation—from Florida to Alabama to Oklahoma, and then back to New Mexico and Arizona when the fight had gone out of them. A visitor to the Apache reservation in 1931 wrote, "The Apache seems completely conquered. . . . His savage spirit is broken. The first Americans who met him found him shrewd, keen, even welcoming; later he proved himself the fiercest fighter in the Southwest. . . . Now he is sullen and uncommunicative, often drunk and lazy."

Today the Apache are beginning to recover from the shock of their defeat. They have many sheep and horses, and are benefiting from gas and oil wells on their land. There are about 13,000 of them, chiefly on two big reservations in Arizona. They are entering the white man's world in great numbers, working as ranchers, loggers, carpenters, policemen, and machine operators. Apache have also specialized in fighting forest-fires, and teams from the Mescalero branch go into action in many parts of the country when fire strikes.

The Navaho, who gave up nomad ways much earlier, have done much better. Theirs is the greatest success story of the American Indians. Today they number more than

90,000, which means that one Indian out of every seven in the United States is a Navaho. They have a strong tribal organization. They are good businessmen, and they have hired shrewd lawyers and administrators to guide them in their enterprises. On their reservation of sixteen million acres they engage in farming, logging, and livestock raising. They have Navaho-owned motels and Navaho-owned curio shops. The sale of Navaho blankets to tourists brings in a sizable income. They have come a long way in the last hundred years.

FROM THE POINT OF VIEW of the Pueblos, the transformation of the Navaho and Apache into law-abiding and prosperous people has been a blessing. For the first time since Basketmaker days, there no longer is danger of nomad attack. The Pueblos have become a people without enemies, free at last to go their own way and follow the traditions of centuries.

Removing the pressure of enemy invasion halted the dismal decline in Pueblo life. For two full centuries, from 1680 to 1880, population curves had pointed downward. Late in the nineteenth century the Pueblos began to recover. The white men had penned up the enemies, and the white men also brought strange new medicines that saved lives. Birthrates rose.

The long agony of the Pueblos, which had begun when the Spaniards arrived, now was over. A happy thriving people, numbering more than 20,000 and living in some seventy towns, had been reduced to fewer than 9,000 in only about thirty towns. The upswing that began some ninety years ago has more than restored all the population losses of those centuries. Today there are about 25,000 Pueblo Indians living in and about the eighteen New Mexican pueblos, and the population is growing by nearly a thousand every year. In Arizona are about 5,000 Hopi on a 631,000-acre reservation completely surrounded by Navaho land.

The best symbol of the new order of things among the Pueblo folk is the change in architecture. For a thousand years the pueblo buildings had no doors on ground level. Nothing but a blank wall ran along the first floor of a pueblo, so that when the ladders to the upper stories were pulled up no enemies could enter. Today every pueblo building has windows and doors on the ground floor. The ladders are no longer taken in, for the enemies are gone.

10

THE LIVING PUEBLOS

In the Southwest today, one anthropologist has written, we can "catch our archaeology live." The Anasazi, the Old Ones, still endure. They have seen the Spanish come and go, they have withstood the onslaught of Navaho and Apache, and now they are trying to hold their own against a new invasion of television sets, tractors, and washing-machines.

Modern mechanical wonders are transforming the Pueblo folk as the Spanish padres never could. A visitor to the twenty-five living pueblos can see at a glance that the old ways are dying. The buildings are still adobe, with that wonderful timeless look, and through the dusty streets of the pueblos run little children and dogs, as they ran in the streets of Tyuonyi five hundred years ago and in the streets of Pueblo Bonito four hundred years before that. The kivas remain, though now most of them are above the surface of the ground.

Yet there are changes. The adobe buildings have glass windows, tin drainpipes, wooden doors. The old many-storied pueblo has been replaced by villages of single-storied or two-storied houses. Television antennas sprout on many roofs. Automobiles and trucks are parked near the adobe walls. The children speak perfect English, and have names like George, Roy, Bruce, Homer, Jane, Mary. There is electric lighting in most of the houses and even in some of the kivas.

The years since the end of the Second World War have hastened the rate of change. More and more, the young people are going outside the pueblo to seek jobs, homes, and husbands or wives. The old languages are being forgotten. The old ways are being lost. Those who stay behind are finding it harder to continue the age-old traditions. For example, the pueblo of Zia has not had a properly elected chief since 1943. In that year the old chief died, and a man named Eliseo Aguilar was named as acting chief. He has never been elevated to full rank, because at Zia the two secret societies qualified to carry out the ceremony have forgotten some of the essential rituals. Similar things have happened at other pueblos. In another generation the age-old ways of the Anasazi will probably have become nothing more than a pretense carried on for the benefit of tourists.

Luckily, the Pueblo culture did last virtually unspoiled into our own time, long enough for dedicated students to record its traditions before they vanished forever. The anthropologists and ethnologists worked side by side with the archaeologists to recover and interpret the Anasazi story. While such men as Richard Wetherill, Jesse Fewkes, and Neil Judd were excavating the ruined Anasazi cities, others were spending years with the survivors of that great age, winning their confidence and setting down an account of their manner of life. Thanks to their work, we know much about the beliefs and customs of the Pueblos, and we can project that knowledge backward in time to give us some understanding of the ancient Anasazi civilization.

One of the first of these investigators was James Stevenson of the Bureau of American Ethnology. In 1879 he went to Zia Pueblo and Zuni to study the social and ceremonial life of the village. He returned in 1887; after his death the following year his widow, Matilda Coxe Stevenson, carried on his work, and extended it to the Hopi. She gained the favor of priests and elders and was allowed to witness some of the most sacred Pueblo rites.

A year after James Stevenson went to Zia, the Bureau of American Ethnology sent Frank Hamilton Cushing to Zuni. He lived in the pueblo for five years. By learning the Zuni language and adopting Zuni ways, he actually became a member of the pueblo. He was adopted into the Macaw clan and was initiated into several religious societies. He dressed in native costume, ate native foods, took part in Zuni rituals. When he left the pueblo he had been made an honorary chief and priest. He brought back a wealth of information, including a Zuni legend of the "black Mexican" who had visited them hundreds of years before—Esteban.

Another early investigator was H. R. Voth. His methods were entirely different from Cushing's. He was a missionary sent by the Mennonite Church to the Hopi in 1901. He built a large church on Third Mesa near Oraibi and attempted to convert the Hopi to his brand of Christianity, but he also spent a great deal of his time uncovering and recording the secrets of Hopi religion. Voth, whom the Hopi called Kihakaumta, "One Who Digs Among Old Ruins," was a forceful, direct man. He would enter the kivas during the ceremonies, carrying his camera. As often as he was thrown out he forced his way back in, until the Hopi gave up and let him watch and photograph their rites. His historic photos and his detailed accounts of Hopi rituals were published by the Field Columbian Museum in Chicago, and remain of great value today for their revelation of the ancient beliefs.

Though the Hopi allowed Voth to study them, and also a man named Alexander M. Stephen who did his work at the First Mesa town of Walpi, they came to resent these intrusions. An "iron curtain" of secrecy was lowered around the kiva, and has never been lifted. Today many of the pueblos allow outsiders to watch their dances and processions, but few visitors have been permitted to enter the kivas since the beginning of the century, and much of the ceremonial is still unknown to us.

Since the time of Stevenson, Voth, Cushing, and Stephen, many anthropologists and ethnologists have visited the pueblos. Hundreds of books have been written on modern-day Pueblo life. Some of the villages have admitted outsiders freely and answered many of their questions, but others remain aloof and tight-mouthed. Thus, although a great deal is known about Hopi and Zuni life, such pueblos as Santo Domingo and San Felipe have kept their ways mysterious. In some of these pueblos the old rites may die out altogether without ever having been revealed.

In this time of change, a constant stream of white visitors flows through the pueblos—not only scientific investigators, but tourists who want to see these islands of an ancient civilization before they are overwhelmed forever by the modern world. The reception that they get varies greatly from village to village. No pueblo is really glad to see outsiders, but some have come to realize that the visitors are important sources of income that can be put to good use by the village.

The most picturesque of the pueblos, Taos and Acoma, benefit from their beauty by charging admission fees. Taos is the only true skyscraper pueblo left. Its two big buildings rise to a height of five stories and bristle with ladders, just as in the long-gone days. Acoma has some three-story buildings and is still located atop its sky-high mesa, although only a few dozen people live there now; the rest have built homes near their fields below the mesa, and return to Acoma only during the tourist season. Both these pueblos charge a fee for parking cars, and a separate fee for taking photographs.

Little Picuris Pueblo, which the Spaniards called San Lorenzo, also welcomes visitors, even posting a sign on the main highway to direct them down the dirt road that leads to the pueblo. At Picuris archaeologists have excavated the ruins of the old village, a few hundred feet from the present one, and for a small fee the five-century-old-site can be explored.

At other pueblos like Cochiti, Tesuque, Zia, and Santo Domingo, the tourists are generally ignored. A few children may come up to say hello in a shy way, a few women may try to sell pottery, but usually the visitor passes through the pueblo without meeting or talking to any of the Indians. A sure way to attract attention, though, is to approach the kiva and try to enter it; instantly stern-faced Indians will appear and ask that you keep away.

It is a mistake to think that either the pueblos or the Pueblos are all alike. They are not. Certain basic things are the same: all are of the same racial stock, they have similar religious beliefs, they are an agricultural people. But the differences are great.

They speak different languages. A man speaking the native language of Taos cannot communicate with a man speaking the language of Santo Domingo any more easily than a Frenchman can speak with a Japanese. Though most of the pueblos along the Rio Grande speak languages of the Tanoan family, there are sharp differences between the dialects, and one large group of Rio Grande pueblos has a completely unrelated language.

The two northernmost Rio Grande pueblos, Taos and Picuris, speak the Tanoan language called Tiwa. That is also the language of the two southernmost Rio Grande villages, Isleta and Sandia. The people of Sandia and Isleta understand each other readily, as do those of Taos and Picuris. But the northern Tiwas have difficulty in comprehending the dialect spoken in the south, although, curiously, a man of Isleta or Sandia can manage to understand the Taos-Picuris dialect.

The Tanoan language known as Tewa is spoken in a group of pueblos south of Picuris—San Juan, Santa Clara, San Ildefonso, Nambe, and Tesuque. Tewa is spoken also in the town of Hano on the Hopi First Mesa, occupied by the Rio Grande people who migrated there late in the seventeenth century. All these Tewa pueblos are very small. One, called Pojoaque, had only a few dozen inhabitants in 1945, and since then has been abandoned. Nambe, Tesuque, and San Ildefonso have populations of two hundred or less. San Juan, though it is bigger, has fallen away from the ancient customs more than most of the other pueblos.

South of the Tewa pueblos are those that speak the unrelated Keres language. The Keresan pueblos are Cochiti, Santo Domingo, San Felipe, Santa Ana, and Zia. Two others are located more than fifty miles west of the main group. These are Acoma, the isolated mesa-top pueblo, and Laguna, the only pueblo founded after the Spanish conquest. Its history goes back just to the late seventeenth century.

One Rio Grande pueblo has a language all its own. This is Jemez, near the Keresan pueblos. It speaks a Tanoan language called Towa. Once there were other Towa pueblos, the most famous of them being Pecos. But only Jemez has survived.

Another pueblo farther to the west also speaks its own language: Zuni, near the Arizona border. The Zuni language may be distantly related to the Tanoan Tiwa-Tewa-Towa, but it cannot be understood by people of the Rio Grande pueblos. Across the border in Arizona, yet another language is spoken: Tusayan, the Hopi language, which is related to the tongue of the Shoshone Indians of the great plains.

There are about twenty villages on and around the Hopi mesas. Some, like Machongpi, Kateshum, Sikyatki, and Tiquiovi, were abandoned centuries ago. One, Awatobi, was destroyed by the other Hopi towns when it embraced Christianity in 1700. Another, Hano, is the Tewa-speaking pueblo founded about the same time.

Six of the villages are ancient Hopi pueblos: Oraibi on Third Mesa; Shipaulovi, Shongopovi, and Mishongnovi on Second Mesa; and the First Mesa towns of Sichomovi and Walpi. Oraibi has practically been deserted, while most of the others are quite small: Walpi had only 71 people on January 1, 1963. Surrounding these are other Hopi settlements built in recent years and not entirely following the ancient design. A good example is Polacca, below First Mesa, which is very much a twentieth-century town. Another fairly recent settlement is Moencopi, fifty miles west of Third Mesa.

Third Mesa itself has some twentieth-century towns, as a result of strife within the pueblo of Oraibi. Late in the last century the people of Oraibi began to divide into two groups, one favoring adoption of many of the white man's ways, the other shunning all new things and calling for a return to the old customs. These factions, the liberals and the conservatives, debated so heatedly that it seemed there might be civil war in Oraibi.

But the Hopi—aside from their destruction of Awatobi—are not warlike folk. They settled their dispute in a typical Pueblo manner. A line was drawn across the top of the mesa. All the liberals gathered on one side of it, all the conservatives on the other. A "push of war" was held. With great shouts and cries the opposing parties heaved and thrust, until Yukioma, the leader of the conservative faction, shouted, "It is done! I have been pushed over the line!"

Yukioma and all his followers, since they had been

defeated, had to leave Oraibi. They moved out in September, 1906, but did not go far. Eight miles north of Oraibi they established the new village of Hotevilla. During the winter there were fresh quarrels among the three hundred people of Hotevilla, and one group broke loose and returned to Oraibi. They were not allowed to remain there. Driven off by the leaders of Oraibi, they founded a second new town, Bakavi, a mile southeast of Hotevilla.

Meanwhile Oraibi was having its own troubles. With the traditionalists gone, the oldest of all Hopi pueblos found difficulties in continuing the annual rituals. Many of its people became Christians and moved away, settling in New Oraibi next door. Today Hotevilla is the center of Hopi religion on Third Mesa, and Oraibi has only some 150 people left.

The existence of so many languages—Tiwa, Tewa, Towa, Keres, Zuni, and Tusayan—among such similar people, probably reflects the dispersion of the Anasazi in the thirteenth and fourteenth centuries. Though we can only guess at the languages spoken in those days, it seems likely that one language was spoken at Mesa Verde, another at Chaco Canyon, another at Kayenta, and so on through Anasazi country. When the Anasazi began to migrate southward at the end of the thirteenth century, each language group may have remained intact. The Keres-speaking people, the Tanoan group, the Tusayan, the Zuni—each tended to drift toward a region where its own language was spoken. And so the little clusters sprang up. There were other languages, too, which have died out, such as the Piro tongue spoken in the southernmost pueblos.

One puzzle is the existence of two widely-separated Tiwa groups, with Tewa and Keres between them. It is thought that the Tiwa-speaking Anasazi started to enter the area around Taos about 900 A.D. Perhaps around 1100 there was a split in this settlement, and some clans went off to found the southern pueblos of Isleta and Sandia. Later, the Keres-speaking Indians may have come in from the west, leaving an outpost at Acoma. This perhaps took place about 1400 A.D. About the same time, Tewa-speaking Anasazi were leaving the Pajarito Plateau area northwest of the Rio Grande, and filling in the rest of the region.

The differences in language are reflected in other ways. The Zuni and Hopi lived in relative isolation; they tended to be passive and fatalistic, and to accept all events as being the will of the gods. The Rio Grande people, on the other hand, became tougher and more forceful than their western relatives, as a result of being exposed to the direct assault of the Navaho, Apache, Comanche, and other warlike tribes. They tried to control events instead of letting themselves be swept along by them.

Taos, the pueblo closest to the great plains, shows this trait most clearly. The people of Taos are taller and stronger than those of other pueblos, indicating that they have intermarried with Indians of the plains. They are good horsemen and hunters, and depend less on their farms than the others. In their religious beliefs they have absorbed some of the ways of the plains Indians. And they are a vigorous, almost aggressive people. It was Taos that began the rebellion of 1680 against the Spaniards. It is Taos today that seems best equipped to benefit from the heavy tourist trade, taking charge of visitors in a brisk, businesslike way.

The Hopi, desert-dwellers in a hostile environment, seem almost helpless by comparison. Those that still follow the old ways bow their heads to the forces of nature without making much attempt to control them. Their psychology is entirely different from that of the Rio Grande people. It is dangerous, therefore, to speak casually of the Pueblos as a single group. They are very closely related people, with much similarity in their outlooks on life, but a careful look shows important differences.

These differences—and similarities—are apparent in their religious beliefs. One basic idea is common to them all: *man must live in harmony with nature.* Rain gives life to the crops, and rain is the gift of the gods. Since the crops are the life of the pueblo, one must observe the sacred rites that insure the favor of the gods. All the year long there are rituals that must be performed—at planting time, during the time when the crops are growing, at harvest time, and after the harvest, when thanks are due. If the ceremonies are neglected the gods will cease to watch over the pueblo, the rain will not fall, the corn will shrivel in the fields.

But there are wide variations from one pueblo to the next in the form that these ceremonies take. The famous Snake Dance is performed only at the Hopi pueblos, Zia, and Acoma. The colorful, exciting Shalako procession is held only at Zuni. Some pueblos have round kivas, others have rectangular ones. Some have only one kiva, others have several. Over the centuries each group has had plenty of time to develop its individual approach to the worship of the gods.

The Pueblos are an orderly people. The heart of their worship is ritual. As Ruth Benedict, an anthropologist who studied the Zuni for many years, wrote, "The Zuni are a ceremonious people, a people who value sobriety and inoffensiveness above all other virtues. Their interest is centered upon their rich and complex ceremonial life. Their cults of the masked gods, of healing, of the sun, of the sacred fetishes, of war, of the dead, are formal and established bodies of ritual with priestly officials and calendric observances. No field of activity competes with ritual for foremost place in their attention. Probably most grown men among the western Pueblos give to it the greater part of their waking life. It requires the memorizing of an amount of word-perfect ritual that our less-trained minds find staggering, and the performance of neatly dovetailed ceremonies that are chartered by the calendar and complexly interlock all the different cults and the governing body in endless formal procedure."

Ruth Benedict wrote that in 1934. Today it is still true to a great extent. The old rituals still are carried out. But they seem to be dying. Too many of the young people have gone to school away from home and have not learned the complicated observances. When they return, they are outsiders. They do not have the rituals in their bones as their fathers and grandfathers did. The old dances continue to be performed, because they are popular among the tourists, but those who watch closely say that the life is going out of them. They no longer have much meaning to the Pueblos, except at conservative villages like Zia and Santo Domingo, and even there the old men are forgetting and the young ones are not learning the ancient rites.

There are Catholic churches at the pueblos, and this is confusing to visitors. Are the Pueblos Christians? They say that they are, that they belong to the Roman Catholic Church. Yet every village has its kivas. Each year the church is carefully whitewashed and the kivas receive a new coating of adobe. The festivals of the Pueblos do not seem to be Catholic ones. The chants are unknown in Rome. What is the explanation?

The answer is that the Pueblos became Catholics to make the Spaniards happy. They realized that the white priests would not be satisfied until there was a church at every pueblo, so they accepted Christianity on the surface. But when the priests tried to make real Christians out of them, they rebelled. After the reconquest, the Catholic Church quietly came to an understanding: no attempt would be made to suppress the old religion, so long as the outward forms of Christianity were followed.

So, as Matilda Stevenson wrote in 1894 after many years of studying the Rio Grande Indians, they "are in fact as non-Catholic as before the Spanish conquest. . . . [They] have preserved their religion, . . . holding their ceremonials in secret, practicing their occult powers to the present time, under the very eye of the church. . . . The Catholic priest marries the betrothed, but they have been previously united according to their ancestral rites. The Romish priest holds mass that the dead may enter heaven, but prayers have already been offered that the soul may be received by Sus-sis-tin-na-ko (their creator) into the lower world. . . . Though professedly Catholic, they wait only the departure of the priest to return to their secret ceremonials."

The same is true today. The Catholic faith has become part of the Pueblo religion. The cross is considered holy, but mainly because it was a holy symbol to the Anasazi long before the first Spaniard arrived. There are pictures of Jesus on the walls of many Pueblo homes, but he is considered just one supernatural being among many, a spirit brought by the white man. The holy days of the Virgin Mary and of the various saints are celebrated, but after the Catholic priest has said mass, he quickly leaves the pueblo so that he will not have to see the masked figures of heathen gods emerging from the kivas to dance joyfully in the plazas. Yet the Pueblo people consider themselves Catholics, and grow indignant at the thought of joining one of the Protestant churches.

Even today, when the flat roofs of the pueblos bristle with television antennas, strange beliefs still grip these people. At Zia there is a secret underground chamber whose roof is sacred ground. Children are not permitted to play on that spot or even to walk across it. Adults, too, keep away. Two posts placed near it prevent wagons from going over it. The only people allowed to enter the chamber are the head of the Flint Society, a secret "medicine" group, and two of his aides. From time to time they enter the chamber late at night, but what they do there remains unknown to the rest of the pueblo and, of course, to all outsiders. When the anthropologist Leslie A. White studied Zia in the 1950's, he obtained much information about the pueblo's beliefs, but no one could tell him anything about the mysterious chamber. One man thought it might contain four small rusty bronze cannon that Coronado gave the pueblo in 1540, but he was not sure.

Every pueblo has its secret places of this sort. Whenever we let the tractors and the television sets fool us into thinking that these Indians are very much like ourselves, we come up short against something that reminds us that they are different, strange, set apart. The cleavage between their culture and ours has been emphasized by Erna Fergusson, a New Mexico woman who has entered closely into Pueblo life and ceremonies. She writes as follows: "Suddenly I knew how alien I was in that Indian world. It is a separate world. The white man sees it, he touches it, some even have the temerity to break into it, to change it. But they cannot. For this is a world apart, a brown world of brown people. They come out of their world sometimes to speak to us, for they understand our language; but when they withdraw into their world, we cannot follow."

Today some of that strangeness is ebbing away. Pueblo boys and girls go far from home, and return wearing college sweatshirts, their heads full of ideas from the outside world. They watch the rituals too—even take part in them—but they are unable to feel the meaning of them as the old people do.

What is that meaning? Erna Fergusson put it well in her book: "Their religion is of earth and the things of earth. I thought of all these brown people whom I had seen dancing their prayers, pounding them with their feet into the earth, which is their mother. Her ways are close to them, even when they are hurt. They understand the earth, they dance their prayers into the earth, and they pray for real things, for sun, and rain and corn. For growth—for life."

Pueblo religion is a community affair. A man does not pray alone. If he fears a dry summer, he takes part in the rain dances. If his child is ill, he sends for the medicine men of the proper society, who cure him (or try to) through ritual. No one in the pueblo remains aloof from the expression of religious feeling without also cutting himself off from the community.

The rites govern everything in life: birth, marriage, sickness, death, the yield of the farm, success in war, safety in travel. The ceremonies are lengthy—many of them take several weeks to perform completely—and usually consist of dramatizations of mythological events dealing with the creation and early migrations of the tribe. The kiva is the place where much of the ritual is acted out. Often the men remain in the kiva for days on end, emerging into the plaza of the pueblo only at the climax of the ceremony for its public part.

There are no full-time priests at any village. The rituals are performed by every adult. Certain men lead, because they are older and wiser in the ways of religion and have been initiated into the secret societies that have the responsibility for the various ceremonies. But when the rites are over, these men who have served as priests return to the everyday life of farming and earning a living.

The only men exempt from work are the *caciques;* the word is Spanish and means "chiefs." The cacique is the spiritual head of the pueblo, a kind of high priest, chosen for a life term by the heads of the secret societies. He is a remote and rather lofty figure in the village, who must not become involved in any quarrels or mix too closely into pueblo politics. The cacique determines the time for each ritual and presides over the religious life of the community, but other men—the heads of the secret societies—are the actual leaders of the ceremonies. In the Tewa-speaking pueblos, each village is divided into two groups, the Winter People and the Summer People, each with its own cacique who presides for half the year. In pueblos of the other language groups, there is only one cacique. He should not be confused with the *governor* of the pueblo, an official chosen by the cacique for a one-year or two-year term. The governor's job is the day-by-day supervision of pueblo life. He handles such things as granting permits to the tourists who wish to photograph the village, and dealing with government officials of the outside world when they have business with the pueblo.

The men who hold power in a pueblo do not seek it. It is considered bad taste to seem to want important responsibilities. The cacique, the governor, the heads of the secret societies, all occupy their posts because somebody must occupy them. They bow to duty. It is unthinkable that a man should campaign for high office the way men do for the American presidency. In the pueblos, office is thrust upon a man, and he accepts it with genuine reluctance. His turn has come, that is all. Since most of the pueblos have populations of only a few hundred, nearly everyone holds important office at some time in his life. The priests and officials are not regarded as having any special authority in their own right, but only by virtue of the offices they hold. A person with power, to the Zuni, is "one who knows how." He is merely part of the great interlocking machinery of pueblo life, and when he relinquishes his power he drops back with relief into ordinary living.

The pueblo ceremonies are carried out by tribal societies, each with responsibility over a particular ritual or part of a ritual. At Zuni there are six of these societies, each with its own kiva, its own officials, its own roll of members, and its own special dances. Other pueblos have other societies. In such pueblos as Zia there are eight or nine societies, but only two kivas. They have private ceremonial houses where their meetings are held and their paraphernalia is stored, and they use the two kivas in turn as the time comes for the performance of their rites. In some villages a few of the most important societies have died out.

The societies maintain strict secrecy about many of their activities, hiding them even from their fellow villagers. Concealment is carried to its extreme among the Hopi. One anthropologist has written that for the Hopi "each ceremony is the 'property' of a certain clan or society to whom it is their special religion, and the members so speak of it. Hence there are a number of Hopi 'religions' jealously guarded from the knowledge of all Hopis. This lack of religious unity has set the pattern of clan disunity in secular matters and has been largely responsible for the rifts and splits contributing to the breakdown of Hopi morale."

The Pueblo child becomes aware of his village's religious life early in childhood. He sees his father going away to spend days or even weeks in the kiva. He hears the sound of chanting and drumming. Then—most exciting and frightening of all—he sees the masked gods enter the pueblo and begin to dance.

The masked gods are known in every pueblo by the Hopi term, *kachinas*. They are an awesome sight as they arrive, weirdly costumed, ornamented with horns or parrot feathers or evergreen boughs, their bodies painted and glistening. Each kachina moves at his own pace: some with stately, somber tread, others leaping and capering, running and hopping. The procession moves about the plaza while the villagers watch in silence. Kachinas armed with yucca-leaf whips drive the crowds back, keep them from getting too close to the dancers, order a man to take off his hat or to put out a cigarette. Those who disobey are whipped, and not gently, either.

The fantastic, flamboyant figures are nightmare creatures, grotesque, terrifying, unreal. To the Pueblos they are supernatural beings who live far away and visit the pueblos to bring rain. The kachina legend varies from village to village in its minor details. The Zuni say that the kachinas live at the bottom of a lake in the empty desert south of the pueblo; the Hopi, that they dwell in the snow and ice of the San Francisco Peaks near Flagstaff, Arizona. All agree that long ago the kachina spirits lived with mankind, teaching hunting and farming and the arts and crafts; and when the people needed rain, the kachinas danced in the fields to bring it. But in time there was a quarrel between kachinas and men, and the kachinas went away to live in their far-off home. Now

Hopi kachina doll

they come back only at festival time, to bring the rain.

The Pueblo child watches these strange beings parading in the plaza. The sight instills an awareness that the spirit world is never very far away. As he grows up he is given dolls that represent the various kachinas. There are more than three hundred of them, each with a distinctive headdress and appearance, and Pueblo craftsmen carve wonderful images of them out of cottonwood. These are not toys. They are part of a child's religious education, a kind of catechism. He learns the names of the kachinas and what they stand for.

When the time comes for a boy to leave childhood,

he learns the secret of the kachinas. He is taken to a kiva by his parents or grandparents when he is twelve or thirteen. Kachinas enter. They carry yucca whips, and they are fierce-looking figures indeed. The boy who is about to be initiated faces them in the close confines of the kiva. One of the older men of the pueblo speaks, explaining the importance of the kachinas to the community. Then the terrified boy is whipped by the kachinas. It is not a painful whipping, but it is a frightening one, for the boy still thinks he is in the presence of supernatural beings.

Then comes the great revelation. The masks are lifted from the kachinas' heads, and the boy sees that the masked gods are really just members of the pueblo, men he has known all his life. It is a little like discovering that there is no Santa Claus. The leader of the group now explains that the kachinas no longer come to the pueblos themselves: they have given the people permission to wear masks and impersonate them. When men of the village don the kachina masks and perform the proper dances, the kachina spirits enter them and rain is brought.

The boy puts on a kachina mask himself. He is handed a whip and told to whip the kachinas. This teaches him that he, as a mortal, will have to perform the duties that he thought were in the province of the supernatural beings. He strikes each kachina four times on the right arm, four times on the left, four times on each leg. The leader tells the story of a boy who came out of the kiva and revealed to his uninitiated playmates the great secret that the kachinas were only impersonations. "The real kachinas came," the initiate is told. "They cut off his head and kicked it all the way to the Sacred Lake where they live. They left his body lying in the plaza."

The boy is now regarded as an adult, and he begins to take part in the ceremonies of the pueblo. Girls are almost never initiated into the kachina cult, though they are allowed to know the secret. Women have a relatively small part to play in pueblo ceremonial life, but they have other responsibilities, for they are, in a way, the heads of the families. The pueblo social structure is *matrilineal;* the houses are the property of the women, and descent is in the female line. When a man marries, he goes to live with his wife's family. His children belong to his wife's clan. The most important figure in a child's life is usually his uncle and not his father, for his uncle, being his mother's brother, is a blood member of the clan, while his father is an outsider. On any important occasion, a man goes to his mother's house—returning to his own clan. There is a bond of love between husband and wife, but it is not as strong as the clan bond that links the generations through the female line.

After he has been initiated into the mysteries of the kachinas, a Pueblo boy may become a member of one of the secret societies. As has been said, there are many such societies, each with its special function. In addition to the rain-making societies whose members wear the kachina masks at festivals, there are medicine societies whose responsibility is the curing of disease.

Few people want to belong to the medicine societies, since membership involves extra work and heavy obligations. A man may volunteer to become a member, but this is seldom done. Usually he is invited to join after the society has cured him of some illness. It is considered bad form to refuse, and, especially if he was seriously sick, he will probably accept. Parents may enroll their children in medicine societies when they are very young, and this is often done when a child is sickly or when a prophetic dream suggests the wisdom of taking special precautions. A family that has had only daughters may vow to enroll their next child in a medicine society if it is a boy. But although these societies have rituals that are supposed to cure the sick, the Pueblos more and more have come to rely upon the government hospitals that have been built near their villages.

The average person is reluctant to join any society, and extreme steps are sometimes resorted to as a means of securing new members. One way to get members is to "trap" them. Imaginary lines are drawn around the headquarters of the society. The head of the society makes a public announcement of that fact and gives warning that anyone crossing the lines will be inducted into membership; and if a person forgets and carelessly walks across the lines, he is immediately seized, taken into the ceremonial house, and enrolled on the spot. Even little children who know nothing about the societies may be "trapped" in this fashion.

Society members have distinct and special functions in the religious life of the community. Some have the privilege of impersonating the kachinas. Others are "clown" societies whose members frolic and cavort during the dances, deliberately breaking the solemnity by playing wild practical jokes on bystanders. At Zuni the clowns are called Goyemshi, "mudheads." They cover their bodies and masks with daubs of mud, and represent the first men who lived on earth after emerging from the sipapu. The Keres-speaking Indians call the fun-making society the Koshare; they are the Kossa among the Tewa, the Chiffonete at Taos. Their function is about the same at all pueblos. They bring to the ceremonies a note of uproarious comedy which seems strange and often out of place to outsiders. The antics of these clowns at the most sacred rituals remind us how different the Pueblos are from us in their attitude toward so many things.

At some pueblos there is a Fire Society, whose ritual includes fire-eating in the best circus tradition. Its members chew the leaves of a plant said to protect the mouth and lips, and thrust flaming sticks into their mouths, extinguishing them before taking them out. Someone being initiated into this society must swallow the flame "raw," without chewing the leaves. "The fire will not burn him if he believes and has faith," an anthropologist was told as recently as 1957.

These fire-eating rituals are performed at Zuni, Acoma, and Zia. The members of the society juggle live coals or bathe in a bed of them. Matilda Stevenson witnessed a Fire Society initiation at Zuni in 1891 and wrote that the initiate "goes to the fireplace and stamps in the fire and literally bathes himself in the live coals. He then takes a large coal in his right hand, and after rubbing his throat and breast with it he places it in his mouth."

The fire-eating is supposed to give the Fire Society members greater powers to cure. Fire is purifying; the medicine men eat fire to acquire its power. Another ritual of this society is sword-swallowing. A curved wooden blade about sixteen inches long is used. It is polished very smooth and rubbed with deer tallow. Sometimes the society members drink a medicine which relaxes the muscles of the throat. They chant and dance, wave the swords high, throw their heads back, and slide the swords quickly down their throats to the full length. The boldest and most experienced keep on dancing even as they swallow the swords, taking a few steps before pulling them out. The sword-swallowing ceremony brings cold rains or snow, and is only performed in the winter.

These various ceremonies are privately held. The few outsiders privileged to see them are anthropologists who have won positions of trust at the pueblos. But certain Pueblo festivals are open to the public, such as the kachina dances. Visitors come from many parts of Arizona and New Mexico and crowd into the pueblos to watch. Most of them have little understanding of what they are seeing, and fail to realize it is a religious rite. They think it is just some gaudy show, like a rodeo. They wander all over the plaza, get in the way of the dancers, and stand in places that block the view of the pueblo-dwellers themselves. Despite the rudeness and ignorance of most of these visitors, they are always welcomed, though photography is strictly forbidden.

Lieutenant James Simpson, who saw so much of the Southwest on his 1849 journey, described Hopi dancing this way: "They keep their elbows close to their sides, and their heels pressed firmly together, and do not raise the feet, but shuffle along with a kind of rolling motion, moving their arms, from the elbows down, in time to the step. At times, each man dances around his squaw, while she turns herself about, as if her heels formed a pivot on which she moved."

One of the first reports of a kachina dance was that of a nineteenth-century traveler named Ten Broeck, who wrote, "Such horrible masks I never saw before—noses six inches long, mouths from ear to ear, and great goggle eyes, as big as half a hen's egg, hanging by a string partly out of the socket. . . . The men of one village would sometimes disguise themselves as elks, with horns on their heads, moving on all fours. . . . Others would appear in the garb of a turkey, with large heavy wings."

A festival that always attracts many visitors is the Shalako at Zuni. It is the great event of the year, held in November or December to begin the cycle of rituals that will guide the village through the winter, spring, summer, and harvest ahead. Preparations begin almost two months before. Those who are to perform visit the pueblo shrines and ready themselves. Four days before the ceremony they disappear into hiding. An air of excitement grips the pueblo. Women bake day and night, preparing corn-bread in their beehive-shaped outdoor ovens. Men drape the houses with yards of gay cloth.

When the big day arrives, the performers slip quietly from their hiding places and leave the village, carrying their masks and paraphernalia concealed under blankets. All day long visitors arrive, always including a great many Navaho who come to watch the ceremony. About four in the afternoon a small boy runs into the pueblo. He represents the fire-god, Shulawitsi, and he is painted black with designs overlaid in red, yellow, blue, and white, the colors of the sun in Zuni lore. He dances for a while. Then a greater god arrives: Sayatasha, the rain-god of the north, draped in white buckskin, laden with jewelry of turquoise, shell, and coral. Hu-tu-tu, the rain-god of the south, follows him, and then two warrior-gods. While they dance, whippers circle about, striking with their yucca whips not only at any dancer who makes a false step, but at any onlooker who might be dozing or failing to pay proper attention.

The dancers sprinkle sacred cornmeal about, and withdraw. It is sunset now, and the Shalako are about to appear. They come around the side of a hill, six giant figures nine feet high, spectacularly huge, dominating the scene. Their headdresses are of eagle-feathers; their faces are inlaid with turquoise. Their feet seem strangely small, for within the gigantic Shalako figures are men. One man carries the huge mask on a long pole hidden under the draperies; another walks by his side, steadying the figure and pulling strings that make the big bulging eyes roll and the wooden beak clack and snap.

The Shalako run to and fro. It is no easy task to run while holding such heavy masks, but for one of them to slip or fall would be a catastrophe for the entire community. The dancers use the skill of long practice in balancing the great masks they carry. They bend their knees, and each Shalako dips until it seems about to fall, and then rights itself. One by one the six towering figures perform, and move on after sunset, each entering a house that has been prepared. If all has been done well, the coming year will bring no calamities. The seeds will sprout, the rains will come, the harvest will be fruitful.

The most exciting and most famous of all the public Pueblo ceremonies is the Snake Dance, which does not make use of any colorful masks or figures. What draws visitors to watch the Snake Dance is not its color, but its strangeness, for it seems to be a rite that survives from an ancient and barbaric past, its origins shrouded in time's mists.

The Snake Dance is performed at Zia, at Acoma, and at some of the Hopi pueblos, but only the Hopi regard it as a public event. The time for it is late summer, when the corn stands tall. Rain is needed now: one last heavy downpour, to see the crops safely through the harvest time.

Two secret societies are involved. The men of the Antelope Society go to their kiva and begin to pray. They gather in front of their altar, which they decorate with a painting of colored sand about four feet square. At each corner of the altar is a "cloud mountain," a small cone of sand with a hawk's feather stuck in it. Ears of corn and bowls of water are placed on the altar. The songs that are chanted are secret, and no outsider is allowed to know them. They tell of the creation of the earth and the migrations of the Hopi. For eleven days the Antelope Society men live in seclusion, reciting these chants.

Meanwhile the men of the Snake Society have been preparing themselves, visiting the Antelope kiva from time to time. On the twelfth day the Snake Society goes out into the desert to gather the snakes. They go in pairs—first to the west, then to the south, to the east, and finally to the north. They carry water jars, sacks of cornmeal, and sacred amulets made from two buzzard feathers tied together. In the desert they search out snakes of all kinds—the harmless bull snakes, the deadly rattlers. No coiled snake is ever picked up. The Snake Society men wave their buzzard-feather amulets over coiled snakes and sprinkle them with cornmeal. They speak softly, addressing the snakes with clan titles. When the serpents uncoil, the Indians grab them swiftly and pop them into buckskin sacks.

The hunters return to the village and carry the snakes to the Antelope kiva. Sand is spread on the kiva floor and the snakes are let loose. There may be as many as a hundred, tangled and twining on the kiva floor—gopher snakes, bull snakes, sidewinders, rattlers. Usually most of them are rattlers. The men sing, lulling the snakes, which slither slowly about. When dawn comes the blessing of the snakes ends, and the reptiles are put into jars.

Other mystic ceremonies follow. It is now the fifteenth day since the rite began. The snakes have been fed, washed, and addressed in song. They are called the "elder brothers" of the Hopi, who ask them to persuade the rain-gods to send gentle rains. On the fifteenth day a race is held between members of the Snake Society and the Antelopes. The winner is blessed in the kiva and receives a jar of sacred water to be planted in his family's fields. The next day a second race is held, and that afternoon is the time of the Snake Dance.

A bower of cottonwood branches has been built in the plaza. Early in the afternoon the snakes are carried from the kiva to this bower and released from their jars. A blanket or a strip of canvas is draped over the entrance to the bower to keep the snakes from escaping.

In their kivas the men of the Snake and Antelope Societies are painting themselves. The Snake Society dancers decorate their bodies with red, white, and black paint. The Antelope men are painted ash-gray, with white zigzag lines across their bodies. All paint their faces white or blue, and wear their hair loose and long.

About four o'clock the crowd in the plaza stirs expectantly. The dancers file into the plaza in single lines. They circle round and round. There is a foot drum in front of the snake bower, and as they pass it they stamp on it to notify the gods that the ceremony has begun. The dull thundering boom of the drum is often echoed by a rumble from the sky, for, more often than not, dark storm-clouds have started to gather over the pueblo.

Now the head of the Snake Society approaches the pyramid of twigs that forms the bower. He reaches in, and when he turns to face the others he is carrying a snake in his mouth. He grasps it just back of its head, with a gentle grip of his teeth. His left hand supports the upper part of the snake's body, holding it level with his chest, and his right hand grasps the lower length of the snake, keeping it at waist level.

He begins to dance through the plaza. By his side is a second Snake Society man who carries a whip made of feathers. He strokes and tickles the snake, distracting it as the first man dances. One after another the Snake Society men take the serpents in their mouths and make the round of the plaza.

When the dancers have completed the circuit and are back at the bower, they remove the snakes from their mouths and place them on the ground. A snake-gatherer now approaches. The snake often is coiled, ready to strike. The snake-gatherer watches it, never touching it. After a while it uncoils and begins to wriggle across the plaza. It may head for the spectators. The Hopi onlookers never flinch or cry out if a snake comes close, but sometimes a white visitor will panic and shriek, or kick at the snake. This can draw a blow from the snake-gatherer's whip. He may even pick up the snake and lash out at the offender with it.

The snakes never escape or bite spectators. The snake-gatherers catch them before they enter the crowd, steering them back with their feather whips. Each snake is picked up, held aloft, and handed to a chanting member of the Antelope Society. He strokes its writhing body and sings to it, soothing it. The dancers take new snakes from the bower and begin a second circuit of the plaza.

The dance goes on and on, until every snake has been danced with. The Antelope Society men may be holding three or four of the twisting, squirming creatures. Some of the dancers have been bitten—for, though they hold the snakes behind the head in a position that keeps them from striking, now and then the snakes twist free and sink their fangs into the body of the man who holds them. A dancer may stagger in pain and seem to lose consciousness as he is bitten; but he recovers, regains his stride, and continues to dance. Some say that the snakes have had their venom-sacs removed before the dance. Others claim that during their captivity in the kiva, the snakes are allowed to strike at small animals, exhausting their poison before the ceremony. Another theory is that the dancers condition themselves by taking small doses of venom regularly. The Hopi themselves provide no explanation, nor do they allow white men to examine the snakes. Many dancers have been bitten, but no dancer has been known to die from the bite.

At last each snake has been carried around the plaza. A group of women has made a circle of sacred cornmeal beside the bower. The Antelope men carry the snakes over and put them in this circle, where they form a writhing mass. They are sprinkled with cornmeal. Then a signal is given, and the Snake Society men rush forward. Each gathers up as many snakes as he can hold. Off they run, down the trail that leads from the mesa-top to the desert. They carry the snakes to the four quarters of the compass and release them. "Elder brothers," they chant, "crawl down in your holes to the underworld and ask the rain gods to have mercy."

At sunset they return to the pueblo. They are given bowls of tea made from a drug that induces vomiting. Standing at the edge of the cliff, they empty their stomachs. Otherwise, they believe, they would remain full of the power of the snake ceremony, and their bellies would swell and burst.

The Snake Dance is over. The skies open, and torrents of rain descend. The dance almost always brings rain, usually within a few hours after the last snakes have been released. In those rare years when rain does not come immediately, it means that some dancer has failed to observe the right ritual, or that there is wickedness in the pueblo.

It is a strange ceremony, a rite that brings chills to the spine of the onlooker. It may have been performed in the broad plaza of Pueblo Bonito nine centuries ago. It may be older than that, going back to the uttermost past of the Anasazi, to yesterday beyond yesterday.

Yet it endures. The next day some of the dancers will be driving automobiles, others will be making telephone calls. At one pueblo there is a new electronics factory where the Indians make parts for the rockets that will carry men to Mars and Venus someday. The twentieth century is rapidly enveloping these people, but still the old rites exist. They may be dying out, but they are not yet gone.

And the Anasazi way may withstand the onslaught of modern civilization after all. These are a people who have weathered drought and plague, famine and war. We who are newcomers to their land come among them and stare at their dusty mud-walled pueblos and at their strange dances and at the sun-baked ruins of their former greatness, and then we nod at the television sets and the shiny cars and tell ourselves that the Pueblos are becoming "civilized" at last.

But they have been civilized a long time. They have lived in their dry, harsh country for twenty centuries or more, and in that time they built a society that had no use for war, a society where every person was important, where the sick and the aging were cared for with love, where the ties of the family were always sacred. Out of the poorest materials, sandstone slabs or desert mud, they built great cities.

They are the Anasazi—the Old Ones. They have survived and endured. And they are still there.

APPENDIX A: WHERE TO SEE ANASAZI RUINS

THE FOLLOWING LIST includes only the major Anasazi sites. All are publicly owned, as national parks, national monuments, or state monuments. Some, however, can be visited only during the summer months because of road conditions. Even during the summer it is wise to check ahead before visiting some of these sites, since rainy weather can make unpaved roads impassable.

ARIZONA

Canyon de Chelly National Monument. Near Chinle, Arizona, on the Navaho Reservation. A spectacular natural setting housing cliff-dwellings and earlier ruins. The canyon is occupied by Navaho Indians. Good accommodations, but the ruins can be visited only in dry weather.

Navajo National Monument. Three widely separated cliff-dwellings on the Navaho Reservation in the vicinity of Kayenta, Arizona. Poor roads lead to Betatakin, a well-preserved house in a large cliff. Eleven miles away by horseback is Keet Seel, the largest cliff-ruin in Arizona.

Still farther away, and hard to reach, is Inscription House. No accommodations except campgrounds, but there are guest ranches in Kayenta and nearby Shonto.

Kinishba. An important pueblo of the eleventh through fifteenth centuries, located on the Apache Reservation near Fort Apache, Arizona. The ruin has been excavated and partly restored. No accommodations.

Tonto National Monument. Two well-preserved cliff-houses of the fourteenth century built by the Salado branch of the Anasazi, near Roosevelt, Arizona. A small museum at the monument, but no accommodations.

Casa Grande National Monument. Immense adobe structure built by the Salado during their occupation of Hohokam territory in the Gila Basin. Hohokam remains are nearby, including unexcavated ball-courts and pit-houses. Museum. Near Coolidge, Arizona.

Wupatki National Monument. Pueblos of the twelfth through fourteenth centuries, and pit-houses. Masonry-walled ball-court. No accommodations. Forty-five miles north of Flagstaff, Arizona.

Walnut Canyon National Monument. Small cliff-dwellings twelve miles east of Flagstaff.

Tuzigoot National Monument. A hilltop pueblo near Clarkdale, Arizona, that has been excavated and partly restored. Good museum of Indian artifacts.

Montezuma Castle National Monument. Impressive cliff-dwelling of the fourteenth century, near Camp Verde, Arizona. Nine miles away is Montezuma Well, with smaller cliff-dwellings. No accommodations, but a small museum at the monument headquarters.

COLORADO

Mesa Verde National Park. The complete story of the Anasazi can be seen here, from pit-house days to the great cliff-dwellings. The Park contains a large museum and many different ruins. Park entrance is on U.S. Highway 160, between Cortez and Mancos, Colorado. From May 15 to October 15 accommodations are available in the Park within walking distance of an important ruin. At other times no lodging, meals, gas, or supplies are available in the Park, but the museum remains open and visitors may drive the loop road on the mesa-top, though the cliff-dwellings can be seen only at a distance.

NEW MEXICO

Aztec Ruins National Monument. A group of Anasazi ruins, of which the largest is a pueblo that once had some 500 rooms. Noteworthy are the restored Great Kiva and the excavated Tri-wall structure nearby. Easily reached from Aztec, New Mexico, where accommodations are available. Open all year. Good museum.

Chaco Canyon National Monument. Perhaps the most important group of Anasazi ruins: more than a dozen large pueblos, including Pueblo Bonito, Chettro Ketl, Pueblo del Arroyo. Small museum, no overnight accommodations. The monument is open all year, but can be reached at present only over unpaved roads that may not be passable in bad weather. On New Mexico Route 56.

Bandelier National Monument. A varied collection of ruins, including the Frijoles Canyon pueblo of Tyuonyi, the small cave-houses, and unexcavated ruins. A lodge providing overnight accommodations is open only during the summer, though the monument itself may be visited all year. Trails lead to back-country ruins; a recommended visit is to the unexcavated mesa-top ruin of Tsankawi, twelve miles by car from the lodge. Bandelier is 46 miles west of Santa Fe.

Puye. Cliff-houses and a partially-restored pueblo on the Pajarito Plateau, not far from Bandelier Monument. Fifteen miles from Española, New Mexico, on the Santa Clara Indian Reservation.

Coronado State Monument. The site of Coronado's winter quarters in 1540–41. Two large pueblos, Kuaua and Puaray, partly excavated and significant because they are the only major ancient adobe pueblos that can be visited. Partly reconstructed, including a restored kiva. Good museum. No accommodations, but easily reached from Albuquerque, eighteen miles away. The monument is just off State Highway 44 near Bernalillo, New Mexico.

Picuris Pueblo (San Lorenzo). An inhabited pueblo two miles west of Penasco, New Mexico. A small but highly-interesting ruined section of the pueblo has been excavated and can be visited.

El Morro National Monument. Sandstone mesa near State Highway 53, about fifty miles southeast of Gallup, New Mexico. Historic carvings of Spanish times, petroglyphs, other inscriptions. Pueblo ruin atop the mesa has been excavated and can be reached by hikers. No accommodations.

APPENDIX B: THE LIVING PUEBLOS

THE FOLLOWING PUEBLOS are inhabited by Indians today and may be visited. They are generally on or near the site of the pre-1540 Pueblo dwellings, except for Laguna Pueblo, which was founded about 1700. Some of the pueblos charge parking fees and additional fees for photography. At others, no photography is allowed. A few of the pueblos have gift shops and refreshment stands, but most do not, and there are no tourist accommodations to be had at any of them. Never try to enter a kiva, a church, or an Indian home without permission.

Hopi Pueblos: Oraibi on Third Mesa; Shongopovi, Mishongnovi, Shipaulovi on Second Mesa; Walpi, Hano, and Sichomovi on First Mesa. In northeastern Arizona; can be reached over dirt roads from Winslow or Flagstaff, Arizona, or Gallup, New Mexico.

Zuni: Thirty-five miles south of Gallup, New Mexico. A large village which has little surviving flavor of the old pueblo style.

Acoma: Sixty miles west of Albuquerque, and fourteen miles south of U.S. 66 on a good gravel road. Spectacularly situated atop a high mesa; tours provided by the Indians.

Laguna: Forty-five miles west of Albuquerque on U.S. 66.

Isleta: Twelve miles south of Albuquerque; most southerly of the Rio Grande pueblos.

Sandia: Twelve miles north of Albuquerque.

Keres-speaking Pueblos: Five villages southwest of Santa Fe. These are San Felipe, Santo Domingo, and Cochiti along the Rio Grande, west of U.S. 85 and north of the town of Bernalillo; Santa Ana and Zia northwest of Bernalillo on the Jemez River.

Tewa-speaking Pueblos: Five villages north of Santa Fe. These are Tesuque, eight miles from Santa Fe; Nambe, sixteen miles north of Santa Fe; San Ildefonso, eighteen miles northwest of Santa Fe; Santa Clara, thirty miles north of Santa Fe; and San Juan, twenty-five miles northwest of Santa Fe. The pueblo of Pojoaque is no longer inhabited.

Jemez: The only remaining Towa-speaking pueblo. About twenty miles northwest of Bernalillo, on the west bank of the Jemez River near State Highway 4.

Picuris (*San Lorenzo*): Forty miles north of Santa Fe and two miles west of Penasco.

Taos: The last "skyscraper" pueblo, with two buildings five stories high. Three miles north of the modern town of Taos, and fifty-two miles northeast of Santa Fe.

FOR FURTHER READING

THIS LIST INCLUDES only a small part of the books and magazine articles that deal with the Indians of the Southwest. I have listed most of the books and articles that I consulted in the course of my own research, many of which are too technical to be of much interest to the general reader who simply wants to know more about the Anasazi than I was able to tell here. I have indicated such technical books with a double asterisk in the following list. Books marked with a single asterisk will be particularly useful to young readers.

GENERAL INDIAN BACKGROUND

* ALVIN M. JOSEPHY, JR., editor: *American Heritage Book of Indians.* American Heritage Publishing Co., New York, 1961.

** ALFRED KROEBER: *Anthropology* (revised edition). Harcourt, Brace & World, New York, 1948.

** PAUL S. MARTIN and others: *Indians Before Columbus.* University of Chicago Press, Chicago, 1947.

* ROBERT SILVERBERG: *Home of the Red Man.* New York Graphic Society, Greenwich, Conn., 1963.

RUTH M. UNDERHILL: *Red Man's America.* University of Chicago Press, Chicago, 1953.

THE SPANISH CONQUEST

JOHN BAKELESS: *The Eyes of Discovery.* Dover Publications, Inc., New York, 1961.

** HUBERT HOWE BANCROFT: *History of Arizona and New Mexico.* First edition, 1889. Reprinted by Horn & Wallace, Albuquerque, 1962.

** A. F. BANDELIER: *The Gilded Man and Other Pictures of the Spanish Occupancy of America.* D. Appleton and Company, New York, 1893.

HERBERT EUGENE BOLTON: *Coronado, Knight of Pueblos and Plains.* University of New Mexico Press, Albuquerque, 1949.

HERBERT EUGENE BOLTON, editor: *Spanish Exploration in the Southwest, 1542–1706.* Charles Scribner's Sons, New York, 1908. (Narratives of Espejo and Oñate.)

BERNARD DEVOTO: *Course of Empire.* Houghton Mifflin, Boston, 1952.

FREDERICK W. HODGE and THEODORE H. LEWIS, editors: *Spanish Explorers in the Southern United States, 1528–1543.* Charles Scribner's Sons, New York, 1907. (Narratives of Cabeza de Vaca and Castañeda.)

PAUL HORGAN: *Great River: The Rio Grande in North American History.* Holt, Rinehart & Winston, New York, 1954.

** WOODBURY LOWERY: *The Spanish Settlements Within the Present Limits of the United States.* First edition, 1903. Reprinted by Russell & Russell, New York, 1959.

GASPAR PÉREZ VILLAGRÁ: *History of New Mexico.*

Translated by Gilberto Espinosa. First edition, 1933. Reprinted by Rio Grande Press, Chicago, 1962.

THE ARCHAEOLOGICAL RECORD

* GORDON C. BALDWIN: *America's Buried Past.* G. P. Putnam's Sons, New York, 1962.

* JOHN M. CORBETT: *Aztec Ruins National Monument.* National Park Service Historical Handbook Series No. 36. United States Department of the Interior, Washington, D.C., 1963.

ANDREW ELLICOTT DOUGLASS: "The Secret of the Southwest Solved by Talkative Tree Rings." *The National Geographic Magazine,* Vol. LVI, No. 6 (December, 1929).

** JESSE WALTER FEWKES: *Antiquities of the Mesa Verde National Park: Cliff Palace.* Bureau of American Ethnology Bulletin 51. Smithsonian Institution, Washington, D.C., 1911.

NEIL M. JUDD: "Everyday Life in Pueblo Bonito." *The National Geographic Magazine,* Vol. XLVIII, No. 3 (September, 1925).

** ——— *The Material Culture of Pueblo Bonito.* Smithsonian Institution, Washington, D.C., 1954.

ALFRED VINCENT KIDDER: *An Introduction to the Study of Southwestern Archaeology.* First edition, 1924. Revised edition, Yale University Press, New Haven and London, 1962.

KENNETH MACGOWAN AND JOSEPH A. HESTER, JR.: *Early Man in the New World.* First edition, 1950. Revised edition, Anchor Books, Doubleday, Garden City, N.Y., 1962.

EARL H. MORRIS: "Exploring in the Canyon of Death." *The National Geographic Magazine,* Vol. 48, No. 3 (September, 1925).

* DOUGLAS OSBORNE: "Wetherill Mesa Yields Secrets of the Cliff Dwellers." *The National Geographic Magazine,* Vol. 125, No. 2 (February, 1964).

J. H. RUSH: "Tree Rings and Sunspots." *Scientific American,* Vol. 186, No. 1 (January, 1952).

ALBERT H. SCHROEDER AND HOMER F. HASTINGS: *Montezuma Castle National Monument.* National Park Service Historical Handbook Series No. 27. United States Department of the Interior, Washington, D.C., 1958.

** R. GORDON VIVIAN: *The Hubbard Site and Other Tri-Wall Structures in New Mexico and Colorado.* National Park Service Archaeological Research Series No. 5. United States Department of the Interior, Washington, D.C., 1959.

* DON WATSON: *Indians of the Mesa Verde.* Mesa Verde Museum Association, Mesa Verde National Park, Colorado, 1961.

——— "Ancient Cliff Dwellers of Mesa Verde." *The National Geographic Magazine,* Vol. 94, No. 3 (September, 1948).

KITTRIDGE A. WING: *Bandelier National Monument, New Mexico.* National Park Service Historical Handbook Series No. 23. United States Department of the Interior, Washington, D.C., 1955.

** H. M. WORMINGTON: *Ancient Man in North America.* Fourth edition. Denver Museum of Natural History, Denver, Colorado, 1957.

** ——— *Prehistoric Indians of the Southwest.* Fifth

printing. Denver Museum of Natural History, Denver, Colorado, 1961.

THE LIVING PUEBLOS

** HUBERT HOWE BANCROFT: *The Native Races of the Pacific States of North America.* D. Appleton and Company, New York, 1875.

RUTH BENEDICT: *Patterns of Culture.* Houghton Mifflin, Boston, 1934.

HARRY CARR: *The West Is Still Wild.* Houghton Mifflin, Boston, 1932.

* PAUL COZE: "Kachinas: Masked Dancers of the Southwest." *The National Geographic Magazine,* Vol. 112, No. 2 (August, 1957).

EDWARD P. DOZIER: "The Hopi and the Tewa." *Scientific American,* Vol. 196, No. 6 (June, 1957).

BERTHA P. DUTTON, editor: *Indians of the Southwest.* Southwestern Association on Indian Affairs, Inc., Santa Fe, New Mexico, 1963.

ERNA FERGUSSON: *Dancing Gods: Indian Ceremonials of New Mexico and Arizona.* First edition, 1931. Reprinted by the University of New Mexico Press, Albuquerque, 1957.

* LAURA GILPIN: *The Pueblos: A Camera Chronicle.* Hastings House, New York, 1941.

* EDWARDS PARK: "El Morro: Story in Stone." *The National Geographic Magazine,* Vol. 112, No. 2 (August, 1957).

* MATTHEW W. STIRLING: "Indian Tribes of Pueblo Land." *The National Geographic Magazine,* Vol. 78, No. 5 (November, 1940).

FRANK WATERS: *Book of the Hopi.* Viking Press, New York, 1963.

** LESLIE A. WHITE: *The Pueblo of Sia, New Mexico.* Bureau of American Ethnology Bulletin 184. Smithsonian Institution, Washington, D.C., 1962.

H. M. WORMINGTON AND ARMINTA NEAL: *The Story of Pueblo Pottery.* Denver Museum of Natural History, Denver, Colorado, 1951.

INDEX

Abiquiu, 194
Acoma, 35, 36, 41, 42, 90, 186, 196, 204, 224, 257
  Bowl using ancient design, *ill.*, 91
adobe, 32, 179
Alamillo, 202
Alaska, 44
Albuquerque, 42
Alvarado, Hernando de, 30, 31, 32, 33
Anasazi (Old Ones), 58, 74, 77, 88, 91, 93, 94, 100, 118, 119, 120, 157, 175, 182, 183, 220
Animas River, 68, 80, 132
Antelope Mesa, 28, 182
Apache (apachu-apachu nabahu), 180, 209, 210, 217, 254
arquebuses, 23
Athabascan, 209
atlatl (throwing stick), 64
Awatobi, 184, 199, 205, 206
Aztec, 132
  Aztec Ruins, ground plan of, *ill.*, 133
  National Monument, 255

Bakavi, 228
Bandelier National Monument, 255
Basketmakers
  Basketmaker I, 79
  Basketmaker II, 58–67, 79, 103, 132
    sandals, *ill.*, 60
  Basketmaker III (Modified Basketmaker), 67–74, 78, 79, 121, 187
    weapons, 72, 73
Bat Cave, 48
Beale, Edward F., 15
Beltran, Fray Bernardino, 36
Benedict, Ruth, 231
Bering Strait, 44
Betatakin, 111, 112, 166, 182
Bernalillo, 32
Bigotes (Whiskers), 30, 31
Black Mesa, 182, 183
Bosque Redondo, 215
Broeck, Ten, 245

caciques, 235
caliche (clay), 180
Casa Chiquita, 118
Casa Grande National Monument, 254
Canyon de Chelly (Suyatupovi), 132, 167, 253
  White House Ruin, 167, 215
Canyon del Muerto, 67, 167
Cardenas, Don Garcia Lopez de, 28, 29
Carson, Kit, 14, 215
Casa Grande, 179, 180, 181, 254
Castañeda, Pedro de, 23, 24, 25, 26, 29, 30, 31, 34, 188
Chaco Canyon, 95, 100, 106, 110, 113, 116, 118, 175
  National Monument, 255
Chaco pottery, *ill.*, 100
Chacra Mesa, 137
Chapin, F. H., 170
Chettro Ketl, 118, 129, 130, 255, Figs. XII and XIII
Cheyenne, 201
Chichilticalli (Red House), 23
Chihuahua, 90
Chino, Marie, 90
Cibola, 20, 24, 37

Classic Pueblo (see Pueblo III)
Clovis Point, 45
Cochise culture, 46, 47
  basketry, 48
  pit houses, 49
Cochiti, 190, 203, 224
Colorado River, 56
Comanche, 192
Coronado, Francisco Vasquez de, 12, 22, 24, 25, 33, 34, 35, 125, 186, 188, 268
Coronado State Monument 256
Cortés, 38
cradles, 77
Cristobal, 39
Cushing, Frank Hamilton, 222

Davis, Jefferson, 15
deflector, 70, 82
dendrochronology (tree-ring dating), 106–115
  tree-ring dating, *ill.*, 109
  Beam HH 39, 113
Developmental Pueblo (see Pueblo I and II)
Diné, 210
Dominguez, 203
Douglas, Andrew E., Dr., 106, 107, 108

El Estanque del Peñol (The Pool by the Great Rock), 13
El Morro (Inscription Rock), 11, 13, 14, 15, 36, 42, 118
  National Monument, 256
El Paso, 38
Escalante, Fray Silvestre de, 207, 208
Espejo, Antonio de, 12, 36, 37, 208
Esteban, 17, 18, 19, 20, 186, 195, 222
estufas (ovens), 38

Fergusson, Erna, 234
Fewkes, Jesse W., 163, 172, 207
First Mesa, 184
  Hano, 184, 227
  Sichomovi, 184, 227
  Walpi, 184, 223, 227
Flagstaff, Arizona, 177
Folsom Man, 45
"Four Corners," 55, 58 63, 69, 72, 77, 95, 96, 158, 175, 180

Gallegos, 35
Garaycoechea, Padre Juan, 205
Garcés, Francisco, 207
Gila River, 52
Gila Valley, 20, 179, 180, 183, 254
Gladwin, Harold S., 52
Gobernador Canyon, 209
Goyemshi (Koshare-Kossa-Chiffonete), 243
Grand Canyon, 29
Great Pueblo (see Pueblo III)
Gulf of California, 42
Gypsum Cave Points, 45

Halona, 186
Hano (see First Mesa)
Hawikuh, 20, 21, 24, 29, 186
Hodge, 187
hogans, 209
Hohokam, 49, 52, 59, 65, 72, 86, 91, 92, 93, 177, 179, 180, 181, 254
  ball courts, 52, 92, 178
  cremation, 163
  irrigation canals, 91
Hopi Tribe (Hopitu-Moqui), 14, 27, 41, 57, 104, 111, 112, 183, 184, 192, 205, 207, 218, 229, 237, 244, 257
  Flute Clan, 131
  pottery, 113, 131
  Snake Clan, 131
Hotavilla, 228
Hungo Pavie, 118
Hu-tu-tu, Rain god of the South, 246
Hyde Brothers, 119

Inscription House, 166
Isleta, 200, 201, 203, 225, 258, Figs. XXII and XXIII

Jackson, W. H., 168
Jemez, 199, Fig. VIII
Judd, Neil M., 119, 125

Kansas, 34
Kachinas, 238
  Hopi kachina doll, *ill.*, 239
Kayenta, 57, 62, 94, 101, 113, 114, 166, 175, 181, 253
  pottery, black on white pottery bowl, *ill.*, 103
  Keet Seel, 166, 182
Kearny, Stephen Watts, General, 214
Keresan, 188, 226, 258
Kern, Richard H., 14
Kinishba, 254
Kin Kletso, 118, 131, 176
Kin Nahasbas, 118
Kino, Father Eusebio, 179
Kiowas, 201, 202
kivas (ceremonial chambers), 11, 37, 71, 82, 87, 88, 96, 104, 117, 128, 130, 135, 184, 190, 198, 200, 201, 231, 233
  Antelope kiva, 247, 248
  Great Kiva, Aztec Ruins, floor plan of, *ill.*, 137
  tri-walls, 137, 156, 166
Kuaua, 256

Laguna Pueblo, 257, 258
Lewis, Lucy M., 90
Little Picuris (San Lorenzo), 224, 256
Lopez, Fray Francisco, 35, 36
Luis, Friar, 34

Macaw, 222
"manifest destiny," 214
mano (hand grinding stone), 26, 47, 70, 88
Martinez, Don Feliz, 14
Masaw, 191
Mason, Charley, 168
matrilineal society, 241
Maya Indians, 53
metate (grinding stone), 26, 47, 70, 84, 87, 88, 124
Mendoza, 18, 22
Mesa Encantada, 187
Mesa Verde, 57, 59, 95, 100, 111, 112, 113, 114, 131, 157, 175, 176, 178, 181
  Balcony House, 172
  cliff houses, 160
  Cliff Palace, 164, 169, 170, 171, 182, Fig. IV
  kiva, floor plan, *ill.*, 83
  Montezuma Castle, 178
  Montezuma Castle National Park, 255
  pit-house, Fig. V
  pottery bowl, black on white, *ill.*, 101
  Spruce Tree House, 164, 169, Figs. I, II, and III
  Sun Temple, 164, Fig. VI
  Two-Story Cliff Houses, 168
Mimbres, 87, 88, 89, 90
  burials, 88
  dish, *ill.*, 89
  pottery, 88
Mimbres River, 87
Mishongnovi (see Second Mesa)
Modified Basketmakers, see Basketmaker II
Mogollon, 49
  Georgetown phase, 50
  Pine Lawn phase, 50
  pit house, side view, *ill.*, 51
  pottery, 50, 72, 73
  San Francisco phase, 51, 86
  Three Circle phase, 87, 104
Mogollon, Don Juan de, 49
Mogollon Mountains, 49
Montezuma, 12
  Montezuma Castle National Monument, 254
  Montezuma Well, 254
Montoya, 40
Morris, Earl H., 68, 155
Mummy Lake, 174
Maranjo, 199

Nampeyo (woman of First Mesa), 185
Navaho, 57, 118, 119, 208, Fig. XXI
Blanket, *ill.*, 216
Navajo National Monument, 253
Newberry, John Strong, Dr., 155, 167
Newspaper Rock, 182, Figs. IX and X
Niza, Fray Marcos de, 18, 19, 22, 23, 24, 186
Nordenskiold, Baron Gustav, 170

Oñate, Don Juan de, 13, 38, 41, 42, 43, 96, 186, 196, 197
Oraibi (see Third Mesa)
Otermin, Governor Antonio, 200, 201

Padilla, Friar Juan de, 28, 34, 198
Painted Desert, 182
Pajarito Plateau, 188
Papago, 181
papas (elder brothers), 26
Pecos ("Cicuye"), 29, 30, 31, 41, 192, 208
Pecos Conference, 105
Petrified Forest National Park, 182, Figs. VII, IX, and X
petroglyphs (rock carvings), 12, 13, 66, 182, Figs. VII, IX, and X
Philip III, King of Spain, 39, 197
pictographs, 66
Picuris, 200, 208, 256, Figs. XVI and XVII
Pima, 52, 181
Piras, 194, 200, 202
Polk, President, 214
Popé, 199, 200, 201, 204
potsherds, 96, 98, 125, 135, 175
pottery making, 99–102, 113, 124, 125, 136, 177, 185, 186
Puaray, 32, 34, 35, 36, 39, 256
Pueblo, 25, 41, 43, 55, 76, 77, 78
Pueblo I and II (Developmental Pueblo), 79, 80, 81, 85, 86, 100, 102, 121, 132, 182, 187
bowl, *ill.*, 98
Pueblo III (Classic Pueblo—Great Pueblo), 105, 113, 136, 176, 182
architecture, 106
Pueblo IV (Regressive Pueblo—Pueblo Renaissance), 181, 182
Pueblo V, 79
Pueblo Bonito, 57, 106, 110, 114, 119, 120, 175, 182, 255, Fig. XIV
Early Bonitians, 122
Late Bonitians, 122
masonry, 122
masonry, Chaco Canyon, *ill.*, 123
Pueblo del Arroyo, 118, 130, 137, 255
Pueblo Renaissance (see Pueblo IV)
Puye, 256

Querechos (Apache-Tonkawa), 33
Quetzalcoatl, 137
Quivira, 33

Red House, 23, 24
refuse heaps, 84, 85, 86
Regressive Pueblo (see Pueblo IV)
religion, 71, 74, 198, 230–252
Rio Conchos, 38
Rio Grande, 35, 56, 118, 187, 192, 200
Rito de los Frijoles (Bean Creek), 188, 189, 190, 256
Roberts, Frank, H. H., 79, 105, 181
Rodriguez, Fray Augustin, 35, 36

Salado, 178
Sandia, 201, 225, 258
Sandia Man, 45
San Felipe, 201, 223
San Gabriel, 13, 40, 197
San Ildefonso, 190, 194, 197, 208
San Juan River, 56, 69, 80, 121, 199
San Lorenzo (Little Picuris), 224, 256

San Pascual, 202
Santa Clara Indian Reservation, 256
Santa Fe, 37, 200
Santo Domingo, 194, 197, 201, 223, 224
Sayatasha, 246
Second Mesa
  Mishongnovi, 184, 227
  Shipaulovi, 184, 227
  Shungopovi, 184, 227
Seven Cities, 20, 186
Shalako, 245
Sherman, General, 216
Shipaulovi (see Second Mesa)
Shoshone, 201
Showlow, Arizona, 113
Shungopovi (see Second Mesa)
Sichomovi (see First Mesa)
Simpson, Lt. James H., 14, 118, 167, 244
Sinagua, 177, 178, 183
Sinaloa, 18
Sioux, 201
sipapu, 71, 82, 84
Snake Dance, 247
Socorro, 35, 202
Sosa, Gaspar Castaño de, 37, 39
Stephen, Alexander M., 223
Stevenson, James, 222
Stevenson, Matilda Coxe, 222, 243
Summer People, 236
Sus-sis-tin-na-ko, 232
Suyatupovi, 132

Taos, 38, 194, 199, 200, 201, 224, 225, Figs. XVIII and XIX
  Pueblo roof structure, *ill.*, 193, Fig. XX
Tavasuh, 212
Tejo, 18
Third Mesa
  Oraibi, 111, 112, 114, 183, 199, 222, 227
Thomas, 39
Threatening Rock, 127
Tiguex, 30, 202
Tiwa, 225
Tonto National Monument, 254
Tovar, Capt. Pedro de, 27
Towa, 226
Treaty of Guadalupe Hidalgo, 214
Trenaquel, 39
tuff (soft rock), 188
Tupatu, 204
Turk, 31, 32, 33, 34
Tusayan, 27, 226
Tuzigoot National Monument, 254
Tyuonyi, 188, 189, 255, Fig. XV

Ute Indians, 167

Vaca, Cabeza de, 17, 18
Vargas, Don Diego de, 203
Villagrá, Gaspar de, 40, 41, 96
Vivian, R. Gordon, Dr., 138
Voth, H. R. (Kihakaumta), 222, 223

Walnut Canyon National Monument, 254
Walpi (see First Mesa)
Wetherill Mesa
  Chapin Mesa House, 174
  Long House, 174
  Mug House, 174
  Step House, 174
Wetherill, Richard, 59, 119, 168
White Dog Cave net, 62
White House Ruin, 167, 215
Wichita, Kansas, 42
wickiup, 211
Winter People, 236
Wupatki (tall house), 178
  National Monument, 254

yucca fibre, 61
Yukioma, 227
Yuma Points, 45

Zaldivar, Juan de, 41
Zaldivar, Vicente de, 41, 42
Zia, 208, 222, 224, 233
Zuni (pueblo), 37, 41, 186, 204, 217, 222, 226, 242, 245, 257
Zuni (indians), 20, 25, 26, 27, 35, 36, 119, 186, 229